A LOCATION IN THE UPPER PENINSULA

ESSAYS, POEMS, STORIES

Jane Piirto

*To Jeanne,
I hope you enjoy this... Thanks!
Best,
Jane Piirto
at the eastern UPISD meeting
8/95*

Sampo Publishing, Inc.
Box 120804
New Brighton, MN 55112

Published by Sampo Publishing, Inc.
P. O. Box 120804
New Brighton, MN 55112

Copyright © Jane Piirto 1994

Second printing, 1995
Printed in the United States of America

ISBN: 0-9632975-4-6

Library of Congress Cataloging-in-Publication Data

Piirto, Jane, 1941-

A location in the Upper Peninsula : Essays, poems, stories / Jane Piirto
p. 232   cm. 23

1. Essays 2. Poems.   3. Short stories.
 4. Michigan—Upper Peninsula 5. Creativity   I. Title

94-068714
CIP

ACKNOWLEDGEMENTS

Many of the stories and poems appeared previously in such publications as *Denver Quarterly, Louisville Review, Sing, Heavenly Muse!, Heartland, Sampo: The Magic Mill, Finnish American Writers, Finnish Americana, Poetry Now, Ohio Writers, Glass Will and Testament, Horizons, Postcards from the Upper Peninsula, Ookooch, Mt. News, Calyx, Juuret Suomessa*

Gratitude is expressed to the Ohio Arts Council
for Individual Artist Fellowships in Fiction and in Poetry

Gratitude is expressed to the Finlandia Foundation
for a publication grant to Sampo Publishing, Inc.

Cover Photo: "Jasper and Hematite on
Jasper Knob: Ishpeming"
Frontispiece photo: "Mather B Mine Shaft from Bancroft
Location: Ishpeming"
by Steven Navarre

*This book is dedicated to
Steven and Denise (of course),
to whom the Upper Peninsula
and their Finnish heritage
are my legacies*

and to Kay

OTHER BOOKS BY THE SAME AUTHOR

THE THREE-WEEK TRANCE DIET

MAMAMAMA

POSTCARDS FROM THE UPPER PENINSULA

UNDERSTANDING THOSE WHO CREATE

TALENTED CHILDREN AND ADULTS

Contents

Preface .... *i*

ESSAYS
A Writing Life 1
A Winter's Tale 4
The Search for Anna Kärnä 78
Da Yoopers Deconstructed 108
The Summer of the Great Blue Herons 212

POEMS
I Will Never Love Anyone The Way I Loved James Dean 10
The Big Birds 23
Poetmother 29
Cancer Morning, Early 33
The Company 38
Eighteen Maple Trees 45
Iron Worker 50
Iron Miner 52
Blueberries 54
Wild Raspberries 55
Sauna 56
Reunion 5
Mushrooms 58
Canoe 60
I'm A New Yorker Now 64
Grandma, You Used To 69
Mummu Sinulla Oli Tapana 71
I'm in the *Helsingin Sanomat* 73
Easter 100
Everywhere the Voices of the Mothers 102
Meditation at Helen Lake, Michigan 106
Nine Feasts 195
Lilac Time 196
Walking To Church on Christmas Eve 197
From a Porch in the Les Cheneaux Islands 199
Crosscountry: Michigan 201
Sunset With Girls 203
It Snowed All Night 205
Song For A Midnight Swim 206

The Baptism 207
The Fight 208
Her Secret Place 209

SHORT STORIES
Snowman 116
Does It Snow in Vietnam? 131
Deer Crossing 143
Grass Fires 151
Blueberry Season 166
Helvi's Sauna 175

A Map of Michigan's Upper Peninsula

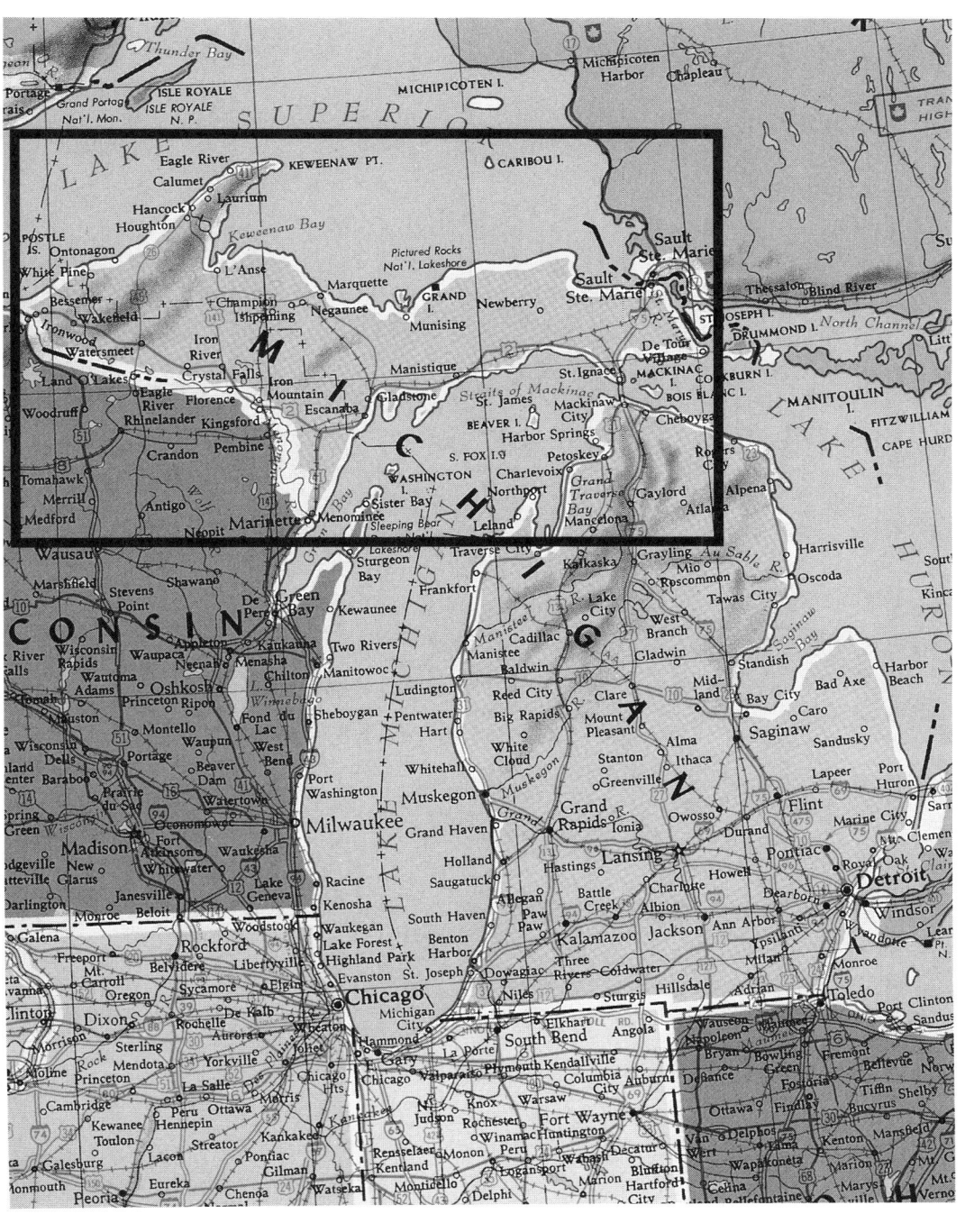

Preface

I am a native of the Upper Peninsula of Michigan, born in a snowstorm just after World War II started. All four grandparents were immigrants from Finland. My father worked in the brownstone shops as a welder for the Cleveland Cliffs Iron Company, and my mother worked as a secretary before and during the War. When we returned to Ishpeming from the Navy Yard where my parents worked in Bremerton, Washington, in 1945, she stayed at home. She was, and is, a very unusual mother—an artist, a reader, a lover of the woods. She was, and is, quite solitary, shy, spiritual, and self-sufficient. Her unconventionality has affected the whole family—my sisters, our children. My father was a loving, gentle soul who didn't even own a deer rifle. He was very inventive and could fix anything. He also struggled with drink, and his alcoholism and its tantrums caused searing memories in my younger sisters' and my childhoods.

We lived in Cleveland Location. A "location," to those who come from mining country, is a settlement of homes built by the mining company near a mine site on land owned by the mining company. My home town, Ishpeming, Michigan, had several locations, among them Salisbury Location, New York Location, Barnum Location, and National Mine Location. Many of the works in this book are set in Cleveland Location. Of course, in choosing the title, I also intended the wider connotation of location as a certain place.

The writer Dan Wakefield conducts a course on spiritual autobiography at retreats, churches, and havens. I took the course a few years ago. During the first lecture in the course, he commented that we all can write an autobiography about any aspect of our lives. We can write our "family life" autobiography. We can write our "friendship" or our "love life" autobiography. We can write our "school and learning" autobiography. These autobiographies necessarily intersect and splash into each other, but the theme, the focus is there.

In some ways, this is my writing autobiography. I have been

given the opportunity to publish my Upper Peninsula writings in this book. How did I come to write them? Why is the Upper Peninsula such a theme in my work? The writer Alan Garganus said that he had to leave the south in order to write about it. Perhaps the same is true for me. I know that every time my car stops at the toll booth on the north side of the Mackinac Bridge in St. Ignace, heading home, my writing self is nurtured. The Upper Peninsula is my psychic and spiritual home.

In 1994, at a reading at Suomi College, John Munson, the editor of the alumni newspaper, *The Bridge*, buttonholed me with many questions. He later wrote a kind article about me. Its title was, "A Writer Looks Homeward for Inspiration," and it said:

For acclaimed poet, novelist, short story writer and scholar Jane Piirto, Michigan's Upper Peninsula holds an almost mystical fascination. 'We all have certain places that seem to stir our creativity,' she says. 'And this is my psychic home—my special place of inspiration.'

Born and raised in Marquette County, the daughter of a Finnish-American welder for a mining company, Piirto became an honor student at Ishpeming High School, studied at Suomi College in 1959-60, and graduated three years later from Northern Michigan University, where she subsequently taught.

Currently, the Fulbright-Hays Scholar is on the faculty of Ashland University in Ashland, Ohio, where she heads the school's program in the education of the gifted and talented.

'Those were memorable times,' Piirto remarked, referring to her years growing up in Upper Michigan. 'Someday I hope to write a book about intuition, creativity, and place, and perhaps explore the importance of this place to me as a creative writer.

'It really is a mystical matter—something I can't entirely explain.'

While she read from a collection of poems titled **Postcards from the Upper Peninsula**—*she revisited her Finnish-American heritage and reflected upon one moment of inspiration years ago.*

'I was driving along the highway when I had the urge to pull over and start writing,' Piirto said. 'The result was a poem telling the story of my grandmother, who, I later learned, had died that afternoon.'

> *... In the field of creative writing, Piirto's accomplishments have included publication of poetry and fiction in numerous periodicals, two Ohio ArtsCouncil Individual Artist Fellowships; poetry and fiction in numerous periodicals, and the publication in 1986 of an award-winning novel,* The Three-Week Trance Diet*...*
>
> *How does she find time and energy to write poetry and fiction in the midst of her demanding teaching, research, and travel schedule?*
>
> *'It's really very simple,' she says. 'When you're a writer, you're just always writing.'*

While I would disagree that my writing has been "acclaimed," I have been invited here to collect some of my pieces and musings about, and set within, this mystical place, this wonderful place, this Upper Peninsula. "Place" has always been important to writers as a concept and as an inspiration, and the Upper Peninsula has always been a place of inspiration, of intuition, and a setting for my writing. This book is made up of essays, short stories, and poems that reflect the Upper Peninsula, and many are in the context of the Finnish American culture as it unfolded in the mid-twentieth century.

I am from what is called the third generation of Finnish Americans, and in my view, our experience is different from that of the second-generation Finnish-Americans, for example, those who wrote essays in Aili Jarvenpa's 1992 book. There is no sentimental memory of the Finn Hall play or dance here, nor of the rural farming community with cows to milk and *pulla* to make, and the predominant language was English, although Finnish was spoken by the parents to the grandparents, or when they wanted to tell secrets. This is not a nostalgic turn down memory lane, nor a romanticized version of hard times. My generation is the generation of the fifties and sixties, and we grew up with rock n' roll, with one foot in the past (pre-television) and one foot in the future (post-Vietnam). Like others in the United States, we have been affected by our generation's pains and trials—divorce, substance abuse, the increase of violence, the vagaries of employment and loss of employment, and a couple of wars.

Today, there are few fourth-generation Finnish Americans, for most of us third-generation "peer" (pure) Finns married outside of the Finnish community, and our children are "half-breeds," as one of my aunts called my children when she met them. I do have two childhood friends who are third-generation Finnish Americans who married third-generation Finnish Americans, but that is more unusual than it is for, say, Italian-Americans to marry Italian-Americans even into the fourth generation, or for Jewish men and women, of whatever nationalities since the diaspora, to marry. My daughter has dark skin and dark hair, and was often thought to have Latino heritage during her school years. "No," she told her third grade teacher. "I am Finnish and I was born in the Upper Peninsula." She has retained her mother's pride in ethnicity even though she is a half breed.

My daughter still proudly puts her place of birth as Marquette, Michigan, even though she has to explain to her fellow New Yorkers where the Upper Peninsula is. My son always telephones me on St. Urho's Day, the day American Finns use as their mythical St. Patrick's Day, March 16, and he wears purple on that day at the photo studio where he works in Colorado. However, being from the Upper Peninsula and being Finnish American does not give worth to these essays, stories, and poems; they must stand on their own, in the emotional truth they tell. They must stand on merit. I hope they do.

I am a researcher and have written a book on creativity, *Understanding Those Who Create*, and so I was interested in exploring my own creativity and its genesis in the autobiographical essay, "My Writing Life," interweaving poems and prose—"creative nonfiction"— in current jargon. An essay called "The Search for Anna Kärnä" traces a search for ancestors in Finland. This first section also includes an essay, "Da Yoopers Deconstructed," about a recent Upper Peninsula phenomenon. The second section is short stories. These stories are part of a larger collection that, like my unpublished second novel, has been a bridesmaid but never a bride in the fiction contests to which we unknown writers submit our manuscripts. I will be relieved to have some of the stories finally collected here. The third section is more poems, some of which have been published here and there, and some of which have not. The epilogue is another essay, "The Summer of the Great Blue Herons," a paean to the wildlife and wild places of the region.

In all, perhaps this book will show that art, intuition, place, and life do have some relationship to each other and will contribute to the debate about the seeds and manifestations of creative expression.

Jane Piirto
Ashland, Ohio

ESSAYS

"Cliff's Shaft"
Photo: Steve Navarre

A Writing Life

My childhood in Ishpeming was spent reading and playing in our woods and minepit-filled neighborhood, Cleveland Location. We didn't call our neighborhoods "neighborhoods" because each had been built around a mine location so we called them "locations." I remember my father and mother talking about buying my Uncle Art's house when he moved to California. This house was across town on Empire Street, near the city playground. The house had a small rocky bluff in the back yard. I worried and carried on at the thought of moving so far (about a mile and a half). I couldn't imagine living in such a citified neighborhood, with just that small bluff, even if it was near the playground and the ice rink and the football field and tennis courts.

Our location had Jasper Knob, which someone had told us was the largest gem in the world, of shiny silver hematite and maroon red jaspillite. It had history. In 1848, Robert Graveraet had left two men, John Mann and Samuel Moody, to guard what was then called Cleveland Mountain protecting, with rifles, one of the first iron ore mine claims. William Burt predicted in 1844 that this area would "far excel any other portion of the United States in the abundance and good qualities of its Iron ores."

Our location had some of the first mines in Ishpeming, iron of such high quality it started a mad rush among would-be metal moguls. We had rocks to climb and pine groves to play in. The nickname of the school system was the Ishpeming Hematites, and hematite is what we had in abundance in our neighborhood. We had maple woods with rutted roads where horse-driven carriages used to take Sunday drives and stop at open air fireplaces for picnics.

We used to play in the woods, imagining ladies in long dresses with wicker picnic baskets and checkered table cloths, languishing in the clearings near the fireplaces. We had the homes and manicured grounds of the mine bosses from the Cleveland Cliffs Iron Company. We used to sneak onto the property and play spy, watching the goings on of these foreign, wealthy, bosses. We took a path through cow fields and cedar swamps to Cedar Lake, where the boys swam naked at the west end of the lake, called Rocky, and us girls swam in swimming suits at Shallow or Pointy on the north side. We had to block our eyes as if we were wearing blinders as we passed Rocky, and a guard boy would lead us by.

Our location had Lake Angeline's bluff, with oak trees and sledge marks from charges driven in to the rock to blast for iron ore. Our neighborhood had Steepie, the finest ski jumping hill in town. Every location had its own ski jump, but we considered ours to be the best. Our neighborhood was the home of the "Flying Finns," the Bietila brothers, world-renowned ski jumpers, who had been ski troopers in the Tenth Division during World War II, romantic figures who fought in the mountains of Italy.

Our location had a summer-long baseball game where the girls were allowed to play too, once in awhile. I had the honor of being the third girl picked, after Linda Lou and Esther. Esther's parents didn't let her play very often, and so I was often picked second. Our neighborhood had The Pines where we played hide-and-seek at night, lying in the shadows of pine trunks, or where we played jungle girls, shouting and yelping like Tarzan and Nyoka.

My parents didn't buy Uncle Art's house across town. We have never been sorry. My mother still lives in Cleveland Location, as do Nelsons, Hollis, Wuorenmaas, Ojas, Jarvinens, Erkkilas, Bietilas, Patrons, Champions, and other long-time Cleveland location families. I go home there several times a year, and walk in those woods, climb those rocks, and sit on top of Jasper Knob.

In my research on creativity and creative people for the books and articles I've written and for the speeches I give, adult creativity is often shown to be shaped by free imaginative play during childhood. Many inventors and scientists, for example, come from rural backgrounds. Being able to play freely, without the invading eyes of adults was a gift of our neighborhood to us.

This tomboy life was also shaped by reading—constant, ceaseless, compulsive, careless reading. When I wasn't playing outside, I was reading. My mother has a sketch of me in my braids, reading *Bill Cody: Hero of the West*. I hated to pose for her so I would read during that boring hour when she would sketch us. I read four, five, sometimes six books a week, all from the Carnegie Public Library on Main Street. I still go there for books every time I come to town, and I belong to the Friends of the Library, devouring their semi-annual newsletter sent to me in Ohio, where I live. I read my way through the children's room where I can still recall the precise spots where the Bobbsey Twin books and the Cherry Ames Student Nurse books were on the shelves. Miss Dundon, the kind librarian with the wooden hand, let me go upstairs to the teenage section and then to the adult section, in fifth and sixth grade. Our parents didn't buy books for us; my mother said that was a waste of money when we could find anything we wanted in the library, and for free. The librarians wouldn't even charge much for overdue books for us readers.

I spent my first allowance, fifty cents, on five comic books at Linna's Drug Store. We kids used to trade comic books, but I was told not to read "love" comics or "war" comics. (I did.) Detective comics such as Dick Tracy were permitted, as were funny comics such as Archie, and superhero comics such as Captain, Junior, and Mary Marvel, Wonder Woman, and of course jungle comics such as Sheena, Nyoka, and Tarzan. My little sister Ruthie, five years younger, loved Little Lulu. She begged me to read her Little Lulu comics out loud to her over and over again. When I lived in New York City, during the 1980s, I was the principal of an elementary school and every year I would tell the students a story about the Upper Peninsula. The city children liked the stories about an exotic land in the far north where we didn't even have television until I was in high school, and then only a black and white movie and the local news. Here is an example of one of the stories I wrote for the children of New York City.

• A Writing Life

A Winter's Tale: Another Story from the Northern Woods

Last year, I told a story about growing up in the north country. You children have been asking for more stories, and so this year I am going to tell you how it was in the winter.

We didn't have TV there, and so we listened to the radio, read a lot, and played outside. Winter in the north is long; we had over a hundred inches of snow, and our favorite sports were skiing, skating, sledding, toboganning, and building forts.

We ski-jumped, cross-countried, and downhill-skied. Our neighborhood had some famous ski-jumpers, The Flying Finns, who had been ski troopers during World War II. In our woods was a long hill called Steepie. These ski jumpers cleared a swath out of the hill and built a wooden scaffold at the top. Then they framed a bump in the middle, hauled all the neighborhood Christmas trees up, piling them into the frame and covering them with snow.

The neighborhood boys let the neighborhood girls "pank" the landing. Panking is sidestepping on skis up the hill in order to make it smooth for the ski jumpers sailing off the bump. The boys let us ride the landing, but they wouldn't let us jump the hill. My friends Susan and Linda Lou, who were good skiers and brave tomboys, used to sneak up early in the mornings before the boys came out. They "stood" the hill called Steepie (that means they didn't fall down).

On Sunday afternoons, the whole family would go "ski-riding" up in the woods along snow-covered paths overlooking high, silent lakes from rock cliffs in pine groves. When we found a good hill we would ride it and climb it over and over. We would have lunch on a frozen log along the trail. It was usually peanut butter and raisin sandwiches with steaming cocoa.

The dog would come along, too. When we fell down in a cloud of snow, he would jump on us as we struggled to get up, and he'd make us fall back again. The snow would get underneath our long underwear and on our wrists and we'd get red, chafed, and cold. Our feet would freeze. When feet thaw, first they tingle, then they burn, and then they ache so much you could scream from the pain.

Our small town of 8,000 had eight ice rinks, one in each "location" (or neighborhood) where there used to be an underground iron mine. The big rink was at the city playground and we went there in junior high to flirt with the boys. The ice rink in our location was about a half mile away, over the hills, and we had to skate there on the snow-covered sandy brown roads, because otherwise we'd have sit in a snowbank to change from boots to skates. That was a very cold changing place, even with the longjohns we wore. We would play Hockey, Figure-skater, Crack-the-Whip, Statues, and Slider. We wore black or brown hockey skates. Figure skates were considered sissy.

"Sleigh-riding" took place on a long, curvy hill, and if we were lucky and the sand truck hadn't come yet, we could ride all the way down to the highway, about 1/2 mile. We would "belly bump" after a big push from a friend who would flop on top the steerer's back. I only made it down to the highway once, but it is a day I'll remember forever.

Our town had a ski area, also, with three slopes and rope tows for each hill, and we downhill-skied in the afternoon and at night. This area, the Winter Sports, as we called it, also had a long toboggan chute. About eight of us would rent a toboggan for about a dollar, and we'd get onto it in the chute shed. The man would tip up the toboggan and off we would go, clattering down the icy chute, way far out, down the hill into the woods. Then we'd tip it over sideways, tumble into the snowbank, and trudge up the long hill again and again. We sure got our exercise.

Snowbanks after blizzards were sometimes twelve feet high, after the plows pushed the snow. We'd dig snow forts and play King of the Castle. The best fort we had had three rooms. Our dad let us take the hose out and ice it so it didn't collapse. One year we and our mother made a beautiful ice throne. She is an artist and can do sculptures that look quite real. The people of the Upper Peninsula have ice statue contests every year. The most famous one is at an engineering school called Michigan Tech.

There were two sports which were quite dangerous. Snowball throwing was forbidden within one block of the school, but I can still remember the warm spot in the middle of my back

• A Writing Life

that I just knew one of the boys would hit like the bullseye of a target as we walked home from school after the one block limit was passed. Car shagging was also popular. You put on ski boots with slick soles and snub toes and lurked in the dark behind a snowbank, and then when a car came by, you grabbed onto its bumper and slid along behind the car.

With all these winter sports and school work too, we didn't have time to miss television. These times were very different from the way we live today here in New York City, but I thought you'd like to read how it was up north.

--from the Hunter College Elementary School yearbook, 1985.

I got decent enough grades, and in junior high was put in what we called the "A" class. Our English teacher, Mrs. Fritz, brought back for several of us, small red Austrian flags from her summer home in Salzburg, Austria, as a reward for learning to diagram sentences the fastest. My verbal interests also extended to the theatrical or oratorical, for I remember our scary principal, Mr. Ikola, inviting my friend Carolyn and me to give our declamations down at the high school, for an assembly in front of the high school kids. Mine was "The Old Woman and the Clock," where I shouted "Ti-i-ick tock, Ti-i-ick tock" in a very dramatic fashion. Both Carolyn and I now do a lot of public speaking, so maybe those early declamations were helpful.

Reading music was also a part of my reading life, and I took piano lessons from Miss Shugren, played clarinet and saxophone in band and orchestra, and sang in every singing group around. Our family were great singers, and we spent many hours singing with our Aunt Siiri or our Aunt Martha playing the good old songs, with Uncle Ernie playing the trumpet, and all the family singing, harmonizing, and knowing the words by heart. We sang everything from hymns to love ballads. My little sister Rebecca learned to use her great big voice early, sitting next to me as I played show tunes and accompanied myself singing.

I also became one of the church organists and my sight reading got a lot of practice because I was lazy and didn't always go to rehearse the service on Saturdays in the darkened church. I would just go and wing it, trying to play a little faster than the stolid Finnish-Americans singing the hymns. They remembered my trying to urge them along, and when I transferred back home after two years of college away, I tried to get my old organist job back, so I would have some spending money. The church council refused, sending the minister to tell me that I jazzed up the hymns too much. But I can still sight read quite well, and enjoy playing show tunes and popular tunes for groups that gather round the piano.

Being a good Finnish girl, doing everything expected of me, my class standing and membership in the National Honor Society was acceptable but not outstanding. There was no hint that I would take up writing, except for my constant reading. I didn't write anything for personal pleasure or expression, except letters. Like most kids, I made several aborted attempts at keeping a diary. Years later, I heard that our high school English teacher, Mr. Renz, had invited some other kids to join a summer writing group. I wasn't invited to participate, so he probably viewed me as not having enough writing talent for such enrichment. Maybe he'd be surprised that I'm the one who turned out to be the writer. We had to memorize a lot of poetry in his class, and I am very grateful. I can still remember sitting in the alto section just after lunch in mixed chorus, memorizing poetry for the quiz in his class next hour. Those words he had us remember are still in my brain. Teachers are reluctant to ask students to memorize nowadays. On another note, the mixed chorus was truly mixed. Boys sang in those days. Now they think it's sissy. I attended church at the Bethel Lutheran church recently and noticed that none of the men was singing. The church used to have a dynamite men's choir with many members.

The influence of the Bethel Lutheran Church was great. Although my parents didn't go to church much when I was little, I was sent, and thrived there. Teaching Sunday school to kindergartners helped me discover my love of teaching. Singing and directing a choir helped me discover my love of music. Attending Luther League meetings on Tuesday nights helped me in leadership. We would have "lunch" at those meetings, and our mothers would send ham and pickle sandwiches or egg salad sandwiches, and brownies or other bars. My mother was a health food nut even back then, and I would beg her to buy white bread for the sandwiches and not to put wheat germ in the date bars. No one would eat them, I told her.

My theatricality on stage (I am still comfortable and rarely get stage fright when I am in front of a class or an audience) led me to be a "singspiration" leader. Singspirations were group singing of gospel choruses: "Hallelu, hallelu, hallelu, hallelujah! Praise ye the Lord!" "For God so loved the world, he gave his only son/ To die on Calvary's tree/ from sin to set us free." I would direct and cajole the audience to sing louder, with more feeling, softer, with more passion, and they would respond. I loved it. I was reminded of these singspirations when I was a school principal and led a school of young children in cheers for our chess team. "Give me an H!" I would shout. "Give me a U!"

Like most working poets, I perform. That is, I do occasional poetry or fiction readings. Usually only a few people come. Recently, I did a reading at the Finnish American Heritage Center at my alma mater at Suomi College. They advertised it throughout the Upper Peninsula; I even saw it in the schedule of events that the Marquette *Mining Journal* publishes. True to form, only a few people came; the professors of literature at Suomi College didn't even come. This speaks to the small interest people have in poetry—at least my poetry. Written or spoken poetry is not important to people, perhaps because poets are not very good performers and often sound pompous when they read, and perhaps because poetry is difficult to apprehend; the listener has to work. When I go to a poetry reading, I often feel awed, as if I am in church, and I let the words just wash over me, not trying to sort out the words and meaning of each poem. That is how I attend concerts, also; I don't analyze the structure of the music while I listen. Just sitting there is a form of meditation. The poetry of song lyrics, on the other hand, has great resonance. People love their favorite songs. I've alternated poems with narrative in this essay so that the poems will be broken up with explanations and anecdotes, and not appear so condensed as they usually are in poetry books. Perhaps you'll find the poems easier to read because of this format. I hope so.

Schools ask me to give speeches on a fairly regular basis, and when I speak with audiences in the midwest, I ask how many people are from the U.P. A few people always raise their hands, and they usually come over to say hello after my speech. When people ask me where I'm going on vacation, and I say, "Home, to the Upper Peninsula," they say, "Is that near Traverse City?" I say, "Go farther north, to the Mackinac Bridge, turn left, and drive about 200 miles." Most can't fathom the distance, the remoteness of this place. But we who are natives of the Upper Peninsula still use our native soil as a badge of recognition. One time a man said to me, "I'll bet you don't know who is the most famous U.S. ski jumping family." I said, "I bet I do." It turned out he had regularly visited his grandmother in our location. As you will see from this essay, The Upper Peninsula is my place even though I don't live there— many others who have to live elsewhere feel the same way.

Another childhood influence was the movies. Oh, I loved the movies. My friends and I would go to the double features on Saturday afternoons for twelve cents plus five cents for popcorn. There would be two black and white movies, cowboy films, and then a serial. Each serial had twelve episodes. There were newsreels and previews of coming attractions beforehand. Each movie was also preceded by a cartoon. I would act out these movies in fantasy play on the bluff across from our house, and would spend days thinking about the plots. Two favorites were *Pinkie*, and *She Wore A Yeller Ribbon*, and later in high school, *Rebel Without A Cause*. I later wrote a poem about my love for James Dean. My mother and father had to make a rule I only could attend one movie a week, just as they had to make a rule that I couldn't read at the table. Now I watch movies whenever I want to, and I read at the table all the time. Here is the first poem in this essay, a poem about James Dean.

Postcard from a Teenaged Girl

I WILL NEVER LOVE ANYONE THE WAY I LOVED JAMES DEAN

in his red nylon jacket at the planetarium
hiding out at the old mansion from that gang
no cause to be a rebel: *I* would have loved him
James—Jimmy—with his sidelong grin those cute
glasses shucks blinks a little wave in his hair
shy shambling no football jock
a poet not a hood

natalie as hot for him as for
splendor with warren
which reminds me of shelley and her tragedy
with montgomery who reminds me of james
dean and there was natalie mothering poor sal as
I would have
and your kisses, James!

I would have helped him too, natalie.
elizabeth after eddie-debbie you are not good
enough for the touch of him my mattress rose
and fell alone in my room with tears for crashes
in crushes in flames of giant lovers in eden

it was the purest love I've known for love's sake
in just 15-year need, the very greed for love
that's unrequited. I murmured prayers to him
before my prayer:

James Dean •

dear james dean james dean don't be dead you can't be dead don't be don't james do james oh james oh.
I took up with Jesus soon after.

• *James Dean*

We were good Christian kids, and got "saved" by Jesus during the summers in high school, at Bible camp at Camp Nesbitt near Sidnaw, and later, at Camp Fortune Lake near Crystal Falls. The fundamentalist wing of the Suomi Synod (most of whom left the Syomi Synod and joined more Baptist-leaning Lutheran branches such as the Lutheran Free Church) seemed to be the leaders at Bible Camp. Other people of Finnish descent were members of the Lastadian, or Apostolic church, and they were not allowed to read the funny papers and had to wear their hair in braids and not wear makeup. But we were the church Finns, following the traditional Lutheranism of Finland. There were also a whole group of Finnish descent people who didn't go to church at all. These belonged to the co-op and to the credit union, and were rumored to be socialists, or even communists, as were "those people in Rock," (a small farm community) as one of my aunts called them. She was a member of the Kaleva Club, a group who wanted to preserve church Finn heritage.

Every summer we in Luther League would go to Bible Camp and during that week we would get saved, declare Jesus as our personal savior. Every fall we would "fall away," to worldly pursuits such as the dances at the Youth Center above Narotzky's car dealership and later at the high school gymnasium. We would dance with the girls to the fast numbers, booming loud Elvis Presley and Gene Vincent. Then, when a slow dance would come on, The Platters or Pat Boone, we would retreat to the sides of the room and hope a boy would ask us to dance. At Bible Camp those fundamentalist Lutheran evangelists would preach hell and damnation to us vulnerable teenagers and scare us—for a little while—a few weeks, a few months.

But one year it really took, that salvation. We were determined not to fall away. It was the summer before our senior year in high school. We came back and put away our tubes of lipstick, our pancake makeup, our perfume. We carried our Bibles wherever we went so we could "witness" or speak about Jesus, to innocent inquirers. One of my best friends was elected to the homecoming court that fall, and rather than go to the dance, she and her date and me and mine, who was on the football team, left after the award ceremonies and drove in her date's Volkswagen bug, in our formal gowns, to the Coffee Cup in Marquette to have coffee and not be tempted with evil rock and roll and darkened school gymnasiums for wicked dancing.

Later I found that the head of the Suomi Synod was very concerned with the hellfire and damnation that those evangelists were preaching to us—this wasn't Lutheranism as it was supposed to be practiced. He was even more concerned because his daughter Marianne was one of us saved ones. She and I carried on a fervent correspondence, writing Christian epistles to each other, deconstructing verses of the Bible from our daily devotions, doing literary criticism before we knew there was such a thing. Later I also found out from a man who had been on the Ishpeming school board at that time, that the superintendent had delegated him to speak to our minister and tell the minister to tone us down. Later, at one of our class reunions, a local boy told me he had always thought I was cute, but I was just too religious. And how. But it was a delicious time, too, a time of purity and a search for truth.

A few years ago, Marianne and I sat down and she read her letters to me that my mother had stored in the attic and had recently returned to me. We looked them over and recognized our searching teenaged selves. My own daughter, then 20, watched us read them and giggle. She couldn't believe we had been so ardent for Christ. Those letters that went back and forth between friends in the late 1950s and early 1960s were detailed, honest, and probing, quite confessional, and above all, indicated the mental searching for truth of our young minds. Too bad the art of letter writing has been subsumed to the telephone, though with e-mail in cyberspace, there's some hope.

Being a child of the working class, and the oldest child, I was the first in my family to go to college, though in the Piirto family it was expected that all grandchildren would go. All my cousins did. I chose my college without counseling or aid. I don't even know if our high school had a counselor, and I missed the testing for the Scholastic Aptitude Test, for some reason or another. I wanted to attend Suomi College in Hancock, Michigan, a Lutheran College of Finnish origins. The reason I wanted to attend Suomi was that one of the most admired girls in our high school, my friend Claire's older sister, Mimi, a church organist and talented pianist (she played Sibelius' "Finlandia" like a pro), had gone there three years earlier. I admired her more than I can say. Also, my admired oldest Piirto cousin Buddy, a Korean vet and former member of Ishpeming's 1950 state championship class B basketball team, was at Suomi, attending seminary to become a Lutheran minister. He had experienced a conversion during this bloody war and decided to study theology. He later became a chaplain in the Navy and was the chaplain on the U.S.S. Hornet when the astronauts came down from the moon. Family mythology has it that he told President Nixon how to pronounce our name: "Peer at your toe. Piir-to."

My year at Suomi was not academically challenging, except for a course from Professor Saarinen called, one semester, "Christian Doctrine," and the other, "Christian Ethics." I had no idea what he was talking about and I loved it. My mind was strained and stretching. I started to read the existentialists and remember struggling through Martin Buber's *I and Thou*, Kierkegaard's leap of faith works, Sartre's *No Exit*, and Camus' *The Plague*. I also remember reading reading reading in my uncritical way, fiction and poetry. I read *Gone With The Wind* for the first time, and a sex education manual a boy named Kenny, who was as baffled as I at the drawings and illustrations, had given me. I had a single room in Suomi's Old Main, and spent many hours reading. I also fed my theatrical instincts by appearing in a play, *The Silver Cord*, as the mother (I always played mothers; I was typecast; there must be something motherly about me; even in fifth grade in the play about the making of "Silent Night," I played Mrs. Franz Gruber. It wasn't until the early 1980s that I played someone glamorous, Lorraine in *The Man Who Came To Dinner*, for the Black Swamp Players in Bowling Green, Ohio.)

At Suomi, even though it was a Christian college, my reading of these dense texts and those wild drinking guys from Michigan Tech, across the Portage Canal in Houghton, caused me to fall away again. I was never popular with boys, and wasn't that year either, and though the great shortage of college age girls in the area led to quite a few blind dates, few of the boys called me back. I even had a blind date for the Snow Ball, with a fraternity boy as shy as I was. We sat silently or made stilted small talk at the fraternity party before and after the Ball. I also remember going to a fraternity house during smelt season for a smelt fry. At that time, I never drank, what with my father's problem and my vow never to be like him, so I'm sure they thought I was quite a prude.

The Suomi College Choir went on a tour to the east that year, and when we Finnish American rural girls saw how short the skirts were in New York City, we rolled up our waistbands and put on more red lipstick. I remember the Staten Island Ferry and the old Finnish church in a rundown neighborhood in Brooklyn. I remember the bus driving out of New York City and me looking out the windows vowing, "I'm coming back to you someday, big city." And I did, twenty-three years later.

That summer I went to Chicago, and worked at Fort Sheridan, 29 miles north of the Loop, as a military pay clerk, GS-2. I met a handsome, tall Italian boy named Louis, from New York City, who was training at the Great Lakes Naval Center. We fell in love and spent all our spare time together for two months. I even signed for him to buy his first car, a 1946 Hudson. I was eighteen and it was legal for me to do so in Illinois. My father thought I was a big fool to trust that he would pay it off. He did, though. I wonder if he remembers that Hudson and my part in helping him get it.

I wrote him a few letters and love poems with carefully chosen lyrics. I still remember our poignant parting on Michigan Avenue in front of the Chicago Art Museum. He shakily drove back to New York City (this was my first city boy and I was shocked that he had just a few months before received his driver's license). I went into the museum and wept in a stall in the bathroom. I would write and rewrite my letters to him, trying to be cool and say it right and not tell him out loud how much I missed him and how much this first love had meant to me. The right words were very important. Erotic love is a great impetus for poetry. Emotion rules and there are few people who haven't been moved to write a few love lines to a love. In the early 1990s, my friend Jim, a philosopher, and I, a poet, put together a reader's theatre piece that we performed in Columbus, Little Rock, and Kansas City, at various conferences. It was small philosophical meditations, poems, and songs, and we ended up calling it "Varieties of Love," for it covered *agape, filios,* and *eros,* the Greek names for love.

I had transferred from Suomi to Augsburg, in Minneapolis, feeling that I wasn't being challenged academically at Suomi and wanting to experience life in the big city. When I got to Augsburg, the academics were very challenging. I began to write more poems and to read poetry books. I remember sitting in a park near the University of Minnesota campus longingly writing a lyric to a boy in my American Lit class on whom I had a crush. The girls in the dorm started to call me "our intellectual," and one girl even gave me a book about science and philosophy that I couldn't understand. I was glad she considered me so smart as to be able to understand this difficult, impenetrable writing. My most pleasant memory of Augsburg is of all of us girls sitting in the dark on the floor listening to Johnny Mathis albums over and over. I also continued my interest in theatre by doing crew on *Diary of Anne Frank* and my interest in music by singing in the girl's choir. The mixed choir was filled with better voices than mine. However, my rural teenage self had been undereducated; in my American literature class, I did a paper on Harriet Beecher Stowe's *Uncle Tom's Cabin,* failing to see its sentimentality. I got a D+, my first—and last.

But times were hard on the Marquette Iron Range, and my father had been demoted from the shops to the diamond drills, where the Company was exploring for beds of iron ore, and so I left Minneapolis and transferred to the state university near my home, Northern Michigan University, where I majored in English.

Life was comfortable. When the car pool picked me up every morning at 7:15 my father would be sitting in the kitchen eating porridge, while my mother packed my father's lunch bucket just as always. My father left for work promptly at 7:20. I had my old room back and spent many hours there reading, writing, studying, mooning around listening to records. The local commuters were the kids I'd grown up with. I barely knew anyone who wasn't a commuter; the dorm and social life at Northern Michigan University, fifteen miles away in Marquette, barely existed. The (I thought then) sophisticated sorority girls and fraternity boys lived lives far from mine, running for office, having parties, attending balls and sporting events. My professors were mostly admirable and dedicated and expected serious work from us. Dr. Barnard, Miss Loubert, and Dr. Rapport stand out. My intellectual juices were flowing and I pasted poems to memorize all over my bedroom walls. "Ah love, let us be true to one another" and "What lips my lips have kissed" and "I saw the best minds of my generation." I thumbed eagerly through the books and anthologies looking for poetic truths.

My first paid writing job was when I was appointed the editor of the college newspaper, *The Northern News*, during my senior year. Before I got the job as editor, I was a feature writer, and it was in that position that I first got into trouble for my writing. I wrote a feature on us commuters, where I used the term "Negaunese," a term one of my drama professors, Dr. James Rapport, used to describe the U.P. dialect that people from the area speak. All the commuters ostracized me. Only Jimmy would dance with me at the Venice and Roosevelt bars in Ishpeming, where we college students hung out, doing the twist on weekends. The next issue of the newspaper was filled with irate responses to my feature. Thirty years later, people still tell me they remember me as that traitor who wrote that article about commuters. I recently reread the article and still view it as a decent attempt at satire being used to argue for social change (e.g., the commuters were being ostracized and ghettoized and the university should do something about it). I was to attempt satire again, when I wrote my first novel years later.

Now I have studied writers in my book, *Understanding Those Who Create*, and I realize that many writers get into trouble for their writing. When they merely think they are telling the truth, they offend people. Kathleen Norris, in her book, *Dakota*, commented on the tendency of local historians to "make nice," to overlook truth and to whitewash, through sentimentality and nostalgia, the struggles of the families of her area, the prairie towns. This is a tendency I try to avoid in my writing. People think my fiction is true, that the stories I tell are stories about me or people I know. Well, they are and they aren't. I have no qualms about altering. Facts aren't as interesting as the imagination. Both my novels are purely imaginative. Writing from the imagination is easier and very freeing. If you write fiction to stick to the facts, why not write nonfiction? It isn't fiction, is it, if you just change the names? As they used to say at the top of those old radio shows, "Any resemblance to persons living or dead is purely coincidental."

This tendency to be frank has not left me as I've aged. I still get into trouble for my writing. I often fire off letters I later regret. But usually I am telling the truth in my letters; my manner of telling is a little too up front. Now, when I speak to high school writers, they often come up to me afterwards and tell me about the underground newspapers they've written for that have been banned when "I was just trying to tell the truth." Recently a review of my book *Understanding Those Who Create* took me to task for saying that some creative people often had lives that were not pleasant, especially writers and actors, and many had suffered childhod trauma. The reviewer, a nice college professor, didn't think that readers should hear such truth, since creativity is supposed to be a desirable thing. Don't shoot the messenger, I told him later.

However, after that spring of being ostracized by my fellow commuters, my friend Susan and I worked in Atlantic City as a waitress and a hostess in a restaurant her uncle owned at the President Hotel. This was before Atlantic City legalized gambling. I don't know what happened that summer—perhaps it was the sea air, and perhaps it was the example of the aggressive New York City and Philadelphia customers we had to serve—but the next fall, my senior year in college, I was not only a player in the political life of the university, for as editor I was expected to write editorials and to have opinions, but I seemed to have gained confidence. Another strange thing happened. The boys started to call. Perhaps they liked this new, confident self which had emerged during my summer in Atlantic City. The English faculty nominated me for a Woodrow Wilson Fellowship and to my surprise, I made it through all the interviews to become a national alternate. I graduated magna cum laude. I remember, at graduation, lining up to go into the arena; my friend Susan was in front—she was summa cum laude. I was in the middle. My friend Judy, who later stood for my wedding, was cum laude, and she brought up the rear of our procession within a procession. During that senior year I wrote poems and more poems and was dating, among others, a poet—an older student, a veteran, who loved literature and taught me a lot. He used to say I looked like Simone Signoret. Boy, I loved that!

That is the same year that the novelist Erica Jong, who attended Barnard College, received a Woodrow Wilson, and she based her novel, *Fear of Flying*, on experiences gained then. I often joke and tell people that if I had gone to Barnard or some other private college, perhaps I would have won a Woodrow Wilson, and I could have written my own *Fear of Flying*. But children of the Upper Peninsula are most likely to choose an Upper Peninsula college—Michigan Technological University, Northern Michigan University, Lake Superior State University—or community college—Gogebic Community College, Bay de Noc Community College, Suomi College—rather than go, as they say, "down below" (the Mackinac Bridge).

Of course, most people are likely to choose a college near home, but I never realized the importance of college choice until I lived in the east. Yes, Virginia, there is an Eastern Establishment. One of the professors on my interview committee down in Ann Arbor at the University of Michigan, the Pulitzer Prize winner Russell Nye, had family in the Upper Peninsula, and he kept telling all those other professors grilling me on my knowledge of literature to let up, "she's just a kid from the U.P." My essay was what got me to the finals, they said. I vaguely remember that essay being about how close reading of the Bible had helped me in close reading of texts. I don't have a surviving copy.

• A Writing Life

That senior year at Northern also introduced me to a professor of modern literature who taught me how to read text closely. Many people reading this will remember Mr. Richer and "Araby" and how we had to read it over and over again. Now, we education professors call his method "teaching for deep understanding." Depth not breadth. He had it right then; after his course I felt I had to go back and reread everything I had read up to that time. The faculty at Northern Michigan University also urged me to change from my major of secondary education and to apply to graduate school with the aim of getting a Ph.D. in English. That was a shocker to me; I had never imagined myself as a college professor; I didn't even know what you had to do to become one. To this working class girl, the professors at Northern were true mentors and exemplars. I did get accepted into all graduate schools I applied to, including the University of California at Berkeley. I would never have believed that I would qualify.

However, I fell in love with a young man from Ohio, who was stationed at the local Air Force base, K. I. Sawyer. We U.P. girls liked the "base guys," as we called them, though some of our fathers wouldn't let us date them. My father didn't mind. And I found those boys exotic and fun. The influence on the U.P. culture of us girls meeting and dating guys from all over the country who were stationed at K.I. Sawyer, has been great. We were going to have a baby so I married this Air Force E-3 radar technician, and I dropped my plans for graduate school for a year. (I went to Europe and Finland with the Suomi College Alumni Choir that summer, while he mustered out of the Air Force. I confided in the nurse on the trip, and she went to a Helsinki clinic and got me those two small pills that give you your period within a week if you are not pregnant. I was. Frantic letters passed over the ocean by air mail. His last one that reached me as we were about to step on the plane in Helsinki, said "I love you. Will meet your plane in Chicago." And he did. We were going to elope, but he said that wasn't right, and we went to his parents, who welcomed me to the family and threw a magnificent wedding for us on very short notice.)

We moved to Ohio, near his parents, in Sandusky. My

writing was confined to a journal about the developmental milestones of this wondrous son, Steven, the love of our lives. First tooth? Two months. First step? Ten months. Allergies? Orange juice. Mr. Richer wrote and told me that one of my poems about some people I knew who chopped up a piano for firewood was going to be in the literary magazine. My first poetic publication. I never saw it. The next year, while my husband started his college education, I picked up my plans again, and we both attended Kent State University. The English department gave me a graduate assistantship, and the first class I taught at Kent was full of men older than I, veterans coming back to school as my husband was. I completed my M.A. in English there, and for one year, taught English, French, and journalism at a nearby high school.

My husband, a hunter and fisher who had loved the area while he was in the Air Force, our son, Steven, and I then moved back to the Upper Peninsula, where my husband continued to study for his undergraduate degree and I accepted a position as an instructor based in the English department, for a new interdisciplinary core humanities program. I loved teaching humanities and writing and the students gave me good evaluations. My dramatic self thrived in a classroom and I got to say out loud all my intellectual thoughts, somehow, while I was teaching.

Another child was born, a daughter, Denise, who is now my best friend. I was glad I had gotten my bachelor's degree before I got married; I had a good job and my salary and the G.I. Bill helped my husband complete his master's degree. Those years in Marquette were heady ones; Northern Michigan University had hired a cadre of young Turks from around the country to teach in its new four-course plan. We partied and talked and we women formed a consciousness-raising group in 1970 to discuss the burgeoning women's movement. Not one woman from that original group is still married to her husband at that time. Our consciousness was surely elevated—or diminished—depending on your point of view.

Among the literary events at the university during those years were several readings by the poet Anne Sexton, a friend of one of my colleagues in the English department. Her work was a puzzle to me. Here was a woman telling honestly the story of her own life. Poets weren't supposed to do that. They were supposed to be objective, scientific, according to the "new critics" who were in vogue when I was in graduate school. I was very moved by her work and her readings, and I studied not only her poetry, but that of her teacher, Robert Lowell. Sexton was a woman and was haughtily dismissed as "confessional" by the critics, though Lowell was as confessional. Another puzzle.

Of course, I've since come to realize all writing is confessional, no matter how the author strives to be objective. This pseudo-scientific/objective stance in the 1950s and 1960s was part of the Zeitgeist of the times. The field of psychology also suffered under such illusion, as the behaviorists took the fore. The field of education also participated, with its "behavioral objectives" and "programmed learning," trying to "teacher proof" curriculum materials. These attempts to be "scientific" tried to take the human out of the process, as if the artist doesn't mold creative work from personal background and insight. In retrospect I realize that Sexton's readings affected my future attempts as a poet trying to tell the truth and not fearing to tell it through her own life.

The Vietnam war was frightening our students as they strove for deferments and grades to keep them legal. We were living in Marquette when the killings of protestors against the B-52s bombing Cambodia happened at Kent State. Being an alumna of Kent State, I was particularly concerned. I remember calling my friend Shirley, who still lived in Kent, and she described the tanks and helicopters roaring around the town. Northern Michigan University students, faculty, and community members had been having sit-ins and had marched around the court house and had had readings of poems and lectures about Vietnam, but it wasn't until 1990 that I wrote this poem about that time from the viewpoint of a teacher who taught extension courses at K.I. Sawyer Air Force Base during the Vietnam war. Here is the poem I read at Kent, for the 20th anniversary remembrance of the 1970 killings.

Postcard from Kent State, 1990

THE BIG BIRDS

*Written for "A Gathering of Poets,"
20th Anniversary memorial of Kent State*

in 1970 the B-52's lined up
at K.I. Sawyer Air Force Base
in Gwinn, Michigan
the Upper Peninsula
were painted sky blue
on their bellies

camouflage green and brown
on their backs
so when they dropped
napalm and bombs
they couldn't be spotted
from below or above

these planes in the Midwest
called Birds
by their managers
stood out huge
in the blueberry forest
on runways on the sand plains

behind chain links on the base
these very planes
flew to Vietnam
through Guam
and the Philippines

reminders to us remote northerners

• *The Big Birds*

of what the pilots and navigators
who lived among us did at work
"We are just in a quiet, dark room"
one of my students, a navigator, said

"Lights blink, gauges beep.
All is quiet. It is very restful.
We get the orders from the ships
find the coordinates
and fly in

"We are so high, miles high
we barely feel it
when we loose the bombs.
Same thing with napalm.
If we bother to look down

"we see a flame
small as a match in a cave.
We're home in a couple of days.
I come to class."

After the killings at Kent State
I went out with my daughter, Denise
9 months old, in the backpack
my son, Steven, 6, at my side
my Another Mother For Peace necklace on.
*"War Is Not Healthy For Children
And Other Living Things"*

collecting donations
in the trailer court
where we lived in Marquette, Michigan
passing useless petitions

to stop the bombing in Cambodia.

Two of my neighbors slammed the doors.
Others gave a dollar, two, five
for me to send somewhere
to some central place

in hope
our children
would not be murdered
when they go to college.
So far it's worked.

• The Big Birds

I taught at Northern Michigan University for five years and then we left, for my husband's first professional job. One of my friends told me that was only just and right, that it was his turn to move for a career. I was sad to leave, and felt my career as a college professor was over even before it had begun, for I couldn't have a real career as a college professor without a Ph.D. I had been given one more year to teach or out, unless I went for a Ph.D. I had hoped to somehow go south to get a Ph.D., at Michigan State or the University of Michigan, or at Marquette University in Milwaukee, though with two small children that seemed impossible. So to South Dakota we went. The existential choice made here was a typical life choice of professional and most women. Mary Catherine Bateson, in her book *Composing A Life*, detailed the uprooting and upsetting and professional compromise of women following their husbands around the world. My life was no different than theirs. And I was glad to do it. In later years, I wrote a scholarly essay called "Why Are There So Few? (Creative Women)" in which I answered that question by noting that women must always operate under the "double bind" of being the childbearer and the caretaker, no matter what. That their creative work, if they are married and have children, is still and always subsumed to their family's needs, and the one-mindedness necessary for dedication to a life of creative production is taken away by the distractions of family responsibilities. I also noted that most women take this path willingly, and, even—instinctually. Working women invariably work the "second shift" at home. Our daughters are realizing that Super Mom is not an easy role to play.

In 1971, with my husband's graduation with his master's degree in regional planning, we left. I haven't been able to live in the Upper Peninsula since 1971, but it continues to be the place I visit several times a year, and I call it "home," as in "I'm going home to see my mother," or "Back home," or "At home we used to . . ." Like most rural areas, the U.P., as we call it, loses its young people to more urban areas. This ended the 26 full years I lived in the Upper Peninsula, for we then moved to South Dakota, where my husband took a position as a regional planner. I had made sure that I obtained my teaching certificate before we left Michigan, but I was "overqualified," meaning too expensive, unhirable at any high schools near our residence of Watertown, because I had six years of experience and a master's degree. I decided to retrain and received another master's degree, in guidance and counseling, from South Dakota State University. I worked as a substitute teacher, and then a high school teacher, guidance counselor, and school public relations administrator, for one year in Florence and one in Brookings. I also had a short stint as a barmaid, saving my salary and tips for a family fishing and camping trip to the Green River (which was set in drab brown) in Wyoming.

The time in South Dakota was a time to look at myself and wonder. The first year there I didn't have a job, and I remember my husband bringing a woman he had met over for lunch. "You'll really like her," he said. I fixed tuna fish salad and wore one of those hostess gowns that were popular in the early 1970s. When they came, I noticed she had great legs in high leather boots below a fashionable miniskirt. I still remember schlepping lunch to them in that nightgown, being the maid while they talked business. That is when I realized I needed to work for my own self esteem, to have some profession besides mothering and wifing. I got a job and have had one ever since.

My sister Ruth has never felt this way, saying her career is to be a mother and wife, and she has always refused to work outside her home while her children Erin, Elizabeth, Rachel, and Moriah were preschoolers, but staying home wasn't for me. I had tasted professional respectability as a college instructor in Marquette. I wanted the kind of validation a career brought. My sister Rebecca, author of two books, and a columnist for *American Demographics* magazine, recently experienced the same depression about her career path when they moved to California for her husband Douglas' job as a plant breeder for a seed company after he finished his Ph.D. and she finished her master's at Cornell. She stayed home with their son Jackson, and was soon expecting another son, Nicholas. Her career was put on hold, except for consulting jobs.

I wanted a forum where I could work out my thinking. I

• A Writing Life

began to write poetry and short stories seriously and to practice writing seriously. By "seriously" I mean that I studied, practiced, attended readings, contacted other writers. When I would go to Minneapolis to visit friends I would haunt the bookstores as before, but now my main buying material was poetry. I was lucky. I saw my first submitted story and my first submitted poetry published in the *South Dakota Review*. The writing became a natural and necessary means of expression and of self-therapy. That is, now that I didn't have college teaching, where, with my speaking and thinking out loud, I worked out my thoughts and ideas, I *had* to write them down. I still use writing to heal myself and to find out what I think about things, even though I have the teaching forum as well. I still spend many hours practicing.

Several other catalyzing experiences happened in South Dakota, which freed me to put my poems to paper. One was participating in an acting workshop with the Minneapolis Children's Theater Company, where I had to fall back into someone's arms, trusting that the person would catch me. This is an old trust exercise, but then it was rather new, and I was afraid. I fell. He caught me. For a shy Finnish American, this was a very difficult thing to do; I couldn't use my words, my verbal aces and barbs. I couldn't criticize and analyze. I just had to trust silently and physically. This experience seemed to free me in some strange and miraculous way, and in ensuing months, the poems poured out.

I told my friends and husband I wanted to practice, practice, practice, and that I would write a poem a day. I remember just after going to bed one night, my husband asked me, "Did you write your poem today?" I hadn't, and so I got up, went into the living room, and wrote a poem about a fly I had killed in the sink. Other workshops in gestalt therapy taken while I got my counseling degree also helped me break through my critical self-censorship to put words on the page and to take myself seriously as a struggling writer. The stresses on the institution of marriage in the early 1970s, where the pill encouraged sexual freedom and experimentation, also played a part in my needing to write it down. One of my first poems illustrates my struggle, as a young mother, to find space and time to be a writer.

POETMOTHER

the afternoon is calm
silence time to write
the paper is green
like the summer

the mind floats into
itself like distanced
birdsong with images
bright as the kitchen sink

the polished coffee table
slowly right there
the words twist from
the images and

the fingers take dictation
fast and willing
then the back door
slaps and his feet
in dirty sneakers tramp

then the voice begins
"Mom where are you
I can't find anyone
to play with

take me fishing
"where's the juice?"
(mom I want)
(mom I own you)
"You can't catch me!"
and the front door crashes

• Poetmother

and a little girl runs
shrieks laughing through
the shatter
I sit up
try again
for stillness

During that time, I had a poem published in a new little magazine called *Jam To-Day*. It was a poem about the last time I saw my father, Christmas of 1973. He died on April 1, 1974. My brother-in-law Bruce called us in South Dakota saying that the time was here, and so I flew to Marquette from Watertown. I remember begging my husband to come with me, and him saying, "I was good to George during his lifetime. I don't need to go to his funeral. I hate funerals." I think that cold statement summarized the way our marriage was going, though it took several more years to freeze up completely. Sitting in the Green Bay airport waiting for the connecting plane, I didn't know whether I was weeping for my father or for my marriage. Feeling very alone, I stepped off at the Marquette airport to Bruce's news that our father was dead. I still feel sad when I type it out. My youngest sister Rebecca was only sixteen when he died, and I remember her running screaming in grief through the church basement after the funeral. She later said she thought that no one was taking this death seriously; they were all being so fake.

Our father might have had a drinking problem, but he was, when sober (every other night), a loving father and a real advocate for us three daughters. He was the eighth child in a family of twelve, and his own father, Herman Piirto, was, from all accounts, a quiet, sober, religious man. My mother, when she started dating my father, would love to come to the loud and bustling Piirto home, because of the presence of Herman Piirto, who was to her everything her own sad, alcoholic, neglectful, absent father was not. My mother even painted a portrait of Herman Piirto that hangs on the wall in her home. She said, "I wished fervently that my father would be like him."

My father's mother, Sophie Piirto, was an archetypal matriarch, large, loving, dominant, and efficient. "She had a mind like a steel trap," one of my aunts said. Another gave me the compliment of saying that of all the nieces I am the one most like her. I adored her and feel privileged that after all the relatives moved out of Ishpeming, I was the one who drove her to church and picked her up. She had a junior high education and managed the family business of milk and dairy products while her husband worked in the mines. She cooked, baked, kept boarders, sewed, kept the good china away in the china cupboard for when the minister would visit. The Piirtos were among the founding families of the Bethel Lutheran Church. In her spare time she knitted beautiful intricate bedspreads of white cotton for each of her six daughters as heirlooms. She gave my mother one, too, and I have it. Even into her old age she continued knitting sweaters for each grandchild.

Our father carried a gentle love with him. He used to call us over and say, "Let me whisper something in your ear." And then he'd whisper, "I love you." After we came from sauna, he'd always say, "You smell like a bar of soap." He always told me, "You're smart. Don't go to Suomi College and Northern to be a teacher. Go to the University of Michigan and be a doctor. Go for the money!" I shrugged his advice off. What did he know about the careers I thought were suitable for girls? Secretary, nurse, teacher, stewardess. My sisters and I now talk about our father with love, and understand that his unwavering love and confidence in us made us know that we ourselves are lovable, that it is possible for us to believe we can be loved by a man.

When I reread my letters home from camp, college, and young married life, I see in those letters a deep love for "Daddy," as we called him. My anger and disdain for his weakness, our lack of respect for him while he was drinking doesn't show in my letters. In later years, my sister Ruth attended meetings of Alanon and she said that I was the angry one, she was the nice one, denying and trying to placate (she suffered from ulcers during high school), and Rebecca was the one who lived with him during the last years, when the ravages of the disease were quite pronounced. To share two memories: he would often leave me and Ruth in the car in winter with the motor running while he ran into the Elks Club for a "snort." We would be there in the darkness for what seemed like hours. Once, when my friend Marianne from Hancock was visiting overnight, we walked up our hill and there was the car up on a snowbank. He had barely made it home. I was shamed and mortified that she would see our family secret in all his disgusting glory. Here is the poem.

CANCER MORNING, EARLY

moths have always fluttered there in your throat,
father, as you lay
skin outlining your skull bones
slack-mouthed, me passing through
your bedroom
my lips just-kissed

on your back snoring always sleeping
like a bald wraith;
but when I kissed you goodbye
your wheelchair bumped the chest
where your underwear
and Mother's

rested in the same drawers clean as always
your frail body always stolidly muscled
leaned up and your whitened whiskers stabbed
my young cheek bent there and I sent the kids
to kiss you too,
and their father

goodbye, we're leaving. *Onnellista uutavuotta*
in freezing dark winter morning of This Is It
the sisters and mother to shoo
the owl I saw blinking on your headboard
the beetles I felt crawling
on my face

    *"Onnellista uutavuotta" is Finnish
     for "Happy New Year"

We moved from South Dakota back to Ohio, near my husband's home, where he took a job working with his father in the furniture sales business. I began work on a Ph.D. at Bowling Green State University. Finally. My work in English at the master's degree level, and my subsequent teaching of English at a university had led me to realize that I didn't want spend my professional life teaching freshman English with its interminable flow of papers to grade, nor did I want to spend my life reading and writing criticism of literature. I know this was nervy to think, but I wanted to write literature, not critique literature.

I decided not to get a Ph.D. in English, but to get one in educational administration and supervision. I thought I could run a school as well as any coach. Besides, an administrator's pay is better. I've never regretted this decision, although my friends and professors at South Dakota State University thought I would be better suited to a field like educational or counseling psychology if I were going to go into education for my Ph.D. I have subsequently written books and articles, and taught undergraduate and graduate students in each of these fields, proving you don't have to have a degree in it to publish in a field or teach about it.

The children and I lived in Bowling Green for nine years; their father lived there for five. They attended elementary and high school there. While in this fine town, I became involved and friendly with the writers, the literary community surrounding the Master of Fine Arts creative writing program at Bowling Green State University— the McCords, Robert Early, Phil O'Connor— and continued publishing poetry and short stories. The Toledo Poets Center founders, Joel Lipman and Nick Muska are also close friends. Other literary experiences were at writers' conferences, the Bread Loaf Writer's Conference in Vermont, and the Aspen Writer's Conference in Colorado among them. The Bread Loaf Conference was rather intimidating and snooty, and the Aspen Writer's Conference gave me settings for future fiction projects and friends with whom I still correspond.

I even founded a small literary press, Piirto Press, that was in existence for seven years, which published sets of poetry postcards and poetry chapbooks. I self-published a chapbook of poems about parenthood, *mamamama* (Sisu, 1976). As a job while I was in graduate school completing my work, and doing research on my dissertation, *The "Female Teacher": The Feminization of the Teaching Profession in Ohio in the Early Nineteenth Century,* I became involved in the National Endowment for the Arts Poets in the Schools program, through my friend Bob Fox at the Ohio Arts Council. I did writer's residencies in Ohio schools in the late 1970s and early 1980s. During those years I also taught as an adjunct professor in the women's studies program at Bowling Green State University and worked in the affirmative action office.

While finishing my dissertation, I was contacted by the placement office. Would I be interested in a position as consultant for education of the gifted programs in Hardin County, about sixty miles away? Yes. I went to the library and read all I could find about smart children (there wasn't much then) and I interviewed for, and got the position. It was February 14, 1977, when I began the day job, the career, I still have today, my career in the education of the talented. Little did I know that call was to be so auspicious. I still am employed in the field of the education of the talented.

I was one of the first funded coordinators in the state of Ohio. I worked in Hardin County for two and a half years, and then I took a similar position, up over the border, sixty miles north, in Monroe County, Michigan, as a coordinator for gifted and talented programs with the Monroe County Intermediate School District. At that time, my marriage broke up. By the time the papers were signed, we had been married almost eighteen years. I remember a poem I wrote my husband for his birthday when we were in our thirties. It said: *1/3 of my life*
I've been your wife

Why did we divorce? From my side of the unbalanced equation, simply put, he broke my heart.

I continued to write and to publish and to be involved in the literary communities of Ohio. I was awarded an Individual Artist Fellowship of $6,000 in fiction in 1982. What a moment that was, opening my mail and seeing that news. That review panel of out-of-state writers didn't even know me! They voted for my talent and they didn't even know my name. I remember taking my children out to dinner at Bowling Green's fanciest restaurant, as a celebration, when the check arrived. But the Individual Artist Fellowship was more than money to free me up to write. It was validation that perhaps I could write that novel I'd been saying I wanted to write.

That summer my children were set to spend a month with their father and his young wife in Port Clinton, Ohio. I was on vacation from the Monroe County job. I thought I'd take a road trip, drive across country all by myself. I mapped out a route that had me stopping overnight with old friends each day, as I would work my way to Port Townsend, Washington, to the writer's conference there. I would have adventures along the way, be a modern, free woman in her car. I might pick up a cowboy at a bar in Montana. Who knew what adventures would befall me? My friends thought it sounded like a great idea. I called my mother, telling her of my plans. She said, in a quiet voice, "I thought you wanted to write a novel. Isn't this a good time to do so, without the kids there?" I ranted and raved about how I have never taken a vacation by myself, about poor me, the single mother, with two kids, working her fingers to the bone, commuting 120 miles a day, and now? What nerve she had to suggest I actually put my fingers on the keyboard and try my skill.

The next morning, I called her at 7 A.M. and said, "You are right. Thank you." And I applied my posterior to the chair, put my fingers on the keyboard, and began.

That summer stands out as one of the most creative in my life. I wrote my first novel, *The Three-Week Trance Diet*, while I was blessedly alone in my own house for the first time, with our Chesapeake Bay retriever, Maynard's, head on my foot. It was the first extended period of solitude I had ever had. I was forty years old and in a state of bliss. I remember writing ten pages a day, every day, chortling at the typewriter as unbelievable, funny, satiric and I hoped, truth-telling characters came out of my mind through my fingers onto my IBM Selectric keyboard. I had the practice of having written a dissertation, and so writing a novel, a sustained project, was not as difficult as I had believed. I couldn't believe that plot was coming out so automatically. Later, one of the reviewers called it "intricately plotted." It must have been all those years of reading novels, novels, novels. I wrote the novel in a month, and the first draft was pretty much the final draft. It was easier than I ever imagined it would be. Where is the tortured writer crumpling up pages and throwing them into the wastebasket, agonizing over each sentence? That writer wasn't me. And it never has been. Still isn't.

I began to send the novel around, hoping to interest a literary agent. No luck. I have never been able to interest a literary agent, although one did contact me when I got the Individual Artist Fellowship. When he found out I wrote short stories, he told me to write novels, novels, novels, and more novels, and then he might, he just might, be interested in seeing my work. I contacted him when I lived in New York City, after my second novel was written, but he wasn't interested. Nor were any other agents. I also entered the novel into the Carpenter Press First Novel contest. Carpenter Press is a respected small press that publishes fiction, one of the few that does. It was their tenth anniversary, and they wanted to celebrate by publishing a first novel. I also put together the collection of poems called *Postcards from the Upper Peninsula*. It was published as a chapbook by Pocasse Press in 1983. The Upper Peninsula was, and still is, magical to me, though I lived in Ohio, and the postcards collection reflected my love for the U.P.

Here is a poem that has been published and, some people say, even xeroxed and passed around. It is a poem about the Cleveland Cliffs Iron Company and the love-hate relationship we have with it. It was first published in *Sing, Heavenly Muse!* Then it was in *Finnish Americana* and *Postcards from the Upper Peninsula*, before it was published in *Sampo: The Magic Mill*. Both the Finnish-American and the feminist literary press have been very good to me and my work, though this poem is neither particularly Finnish-American, nor feminist.

THE COMPANY

I.
Negaunee caves in.
they're moving Palmer.
Republic used to be a bluff.
Ishpeming has no tax revenues
now the undergrounds have closed
Tilden Location is now a metropolis
Cliff's Drive is blocked off
with open pit low grade iron pellets

in 75 years
the largest gem in the world
Jasper Knob
of jaspillite and hematite
will be an open pit too
but they don't call it
strip mining.

here's to The Company!

Mr. Mather and his friends
explored and coveted
they bought and litigated
claimed from the Chippewa

and the word went
New England and Europe
to the famished of famine
Cornish, Irish, French-Canadian,
Swedes, Norwegians,
Finns and Italians later.

poor people
second sons unmarried daughters
sailed to Ellis huddled
carriage canal and railroad
boat and hope
carried them to Ishpeming, Michigan,
where their cousins worked.

housemaids and miners
housemaids and lumberers
housemaids and carpenters
shoemakers merchants farmers
barkeeps and miners
and miners' sons

sought respectability
in claimed cedar swamps
bearing
babies and an ethic
work and not welfare
damp mines and falling chunks
the ore to make the autos
to make America
what it is

compasses went crazy
north pointed south
at this iron red

dust soiled the sheets
hand-wrung, hung
on clotheslines frozen

• The Company

stiff as walls

between workers and bosses
ore
red mud covered sensible
boots tramping trails
in mosquito-owned woods

adventurers became family men
housemaids housewives
and there were children
and hope for the children
and the Lutheran church
and the Catholic church
and the Methodists
and the streets of taverns
and The Company
tentacled.

II.
we are yours, Company.
you pollute with our blessing
you own the land

you hired our grandfathers
our fathers
brothers husbands

you gave us girls college
at Northern and
"teaching is a good job
for a woman"
you own the land

The Company •

our sons go to Northern too
they live in Detroit now
work for the auto companies
or hamburger franchisers
teach school
if they don't work for you
'cause The Company pays good
now there's unions
and being a miner
is a respectable job
and we work for you
whatever we do

III.
my dad died of cancer
he worked in your shops
the noise made him deaf
The Company paid the bills
my mother is a widow
with a small pension
now there's unions

my husband worked the Empire Mine
he spit taconite
black ooze on the pillow
for a year after he quit

but he made good money
saved up for college
my cousin's your accountant

we are yours, Company

• The Company

you showed us the land
your land
seduces us
trout deer waterfalls
clean water pine woods
you only pollute a little
you sent our kids to college
you helped us own our homes
we had nothing
when we came
you own the land
our homes stand on
you hire us
to move our homes
when you wish
to dig a shaft
a pit
a strip
you own the land
and jobs
are more important
than land
we are yours
wrapped and fenced

we are your
links in the chain
pass it on

The Company

I wrote that one night, late, sitting up in my mother's living room, in the late 1970s. At the time "The Company" was published in the chapbook, the year 1982-1983, I was also appointed to the literature panel of the Ohio Arts Council, where we read grant proposals by small presses and literary journals, and helped to fund them. This was a lesson in the frustrations small presses have in publishing and staying afloat, especially small presses that publish fiction and poetry. Then, in the late 1980s, I wrote a companion poem about the company, called "Eighteen Maple Trees." It was published in a Cleveland, Ohio literary tabloid after I read it at a reading at Cleveland State University.

People in the city of Cleveland don't know much about the Cleveland Cliffs Iron Company and its importance to Marquette County in Michigan. I once had a date with a steel executive, and he filled me in on the economics of the steel industry and the very small place our company, the Cleveland Cliffs Iron Company, has in those economics. It put things into perspective for me. This world of the residents in the U.P. is really a very small piece of the world-wide iron mining puzzle in the complex world of steel.

I remember sitting in the Huron Yacht Club with my in-laws, watching the ore boats unload at the Huron, Ohio, pier and thinking, my friends and family mined that ore. The extractive industries have used the Upper Peninsula since its discovery—even the Indians used to travel great distances for the float copper, which they mined in primitive pits in the Copper Country on the Upper Peninsula's Keweenaw Peninsula. That copper may have been traded all over the world by the aboriginal people. Similar copper with the same proportions of other minerals was found in China. The ancient copper diggers used hammer stones to extract the copper from many small pits, some even found on Isle Royale.

The fishing, logging, and mining industries, the bread and butter of the immigrants who were enticed to the Upper Peninsula to work in those industries, feel few qualms about get in, get out, and cut your losses policies; the companies are based in more accessible areas, and the immigrants' children, who now call themselves "natives," are often forced to emigrate from the area.

• *A Writer's Life*

The recent loss of the K.I. Sawyer Air Force Base is another example of the transitory nature of employment opportunities in the Upper Peninsula. I've talked to several people who view the closing thus: "We got along before the Base, and we'll get along after it goes. Good riddance. Now we can keep our daughters home." No one owns a job on or within the land that is owned by the company. Our grandfathers and grandmothers understood that when they braved isolation and the unknown to come to the land and it's interesting that we, their grandchildren, feel an entitlement. The land endures in its shifting forms. Who owns the land matters. Now there is controversy about a large timber company which has bought up many acres in the Upper Peninsula and is clear-cutting within the forests and fencing in access to Lake Superior. Another chapter in an old story of who owns the Upper Peninsula. "The Company" does, of course.

My friend for—at this writing—twenty-six years, my former office mate when we were young, pregnant professors at Northern Michigan University, Kay, who is still a professor in the English department there, is my buddy for numerous expeditions we conduct when I visit the Upper Peninsula. She is, more than anyone, my hiking, lake-swimming, ski-tramping, nature-walking, 4-wheel drive truck, U.P. backwoods safari friend, a fellow native of Marquette County. She says that while bald eagles are now found in abundance in the Upper Peninsula, The Company near her camp, a paper company, is cutting at will on the company's land, using the "selective cutting" technique, they call it, where they top big-circumferenced trees, leaving huge, leafy tops on the ground of the woods to just rot while they harvest the trunks. She said she called the U.S. Forest Service to ask whether there were any regulations about how companies can cut trees, and the officer said, "No." Private property is private property. You can do anything with your forested or ored private property in the Upper Peninsula—and in most oiled areas of the world, also. Many of our wilderness areas are owned by private extractors who hire the local people—who are in a double bind—work and stay here or don't work and can't live here.

Postcard from Jasper Street
EIGHTEEN MAPLE TREES

I call the city manager
to ask who cut down
18 maple trees
on our street,
the oldest street in town
the one with the stone wall

she says, "What trees?
No one has called to miss
18 maple trees
except you and you don't
live here anymore.
You say they were cut down
the end of last summer?
The City of Ishpeming
only cut down 14 trees.
Only one was on Jasper Street.
They had to be cut by
The Cleveland Cliffs Iron Company.
They own all the land."

I call the company, CCI.
"Who cut down the trees?"
"What trees?" the p.r. man says.

Don was in high school
2 years ahead of me.
Head of the Chamber of Commerce
Certainly he cares about
18 maple trees.

• *Eighteen Maple Trees*

"It wasn't C.C.I.
that I'm aware of."
I ask the neighbors
"When were the maples cut down?"
No one seems to remember.
Maybe last summer maybe not.

Neighbor Paulie says he heard
Arvo requested they be cut down.
With all the skiers coming up
to the new ski trail,
the branches fell on the street
after snowstorms.
"it was dangerous."

"Why can Arvo request such a thing
and they would just do it?

"Don't the neighbors
need to know?"
We can't ask Arvo.
Arvo fell off his roof
cleaning ice
he died last year
Paulie says he'll ask
the city crew if they did it

I check the stumps
count the rings
stop at 90
dense and not diseased

I ask Paulette

a neighbor who's a teacher
in the health food co-op
with my mother
"They were just gone
one day at the end
of last summer."

There have always been
changes in the woods
where The Company
mines iron in open pits
we hear heavy machinery
boom through the forests
blasts like earthquakes
echo in the sky

but we, blithe
pick blueberries
we go tobogganing
celebrate family fests
hunt and orienteer
ski crosscountry hills
we swim in fresh spring-fed lakes
we forget—forgive the rampage
of necessary commerce:
The Company

just behind Lake Ogden
a gaping mine in the earth
miles wide and very deep
the red earth yields low-grade iron
for pellets for steel
only seen by nonminers
from commuter planes

• *Eighteen Maple Trees*

when the weather is good
now The Company has blocked off
Cliff's Drive; all gashing is hidden

Ogden flows into Lake Sally
the town's water supply
they changed the water supply
to Teal Lake and then to wells last year.
Sally and Ogden
drop in levels month by month
the mine is two miles
from our home.
 The Company
owns the land.

I ask my mother
"Why didn't you complain
about the missing trees?"

"I assumed
they had a reason," she says.
"I feel
like a collaborator
with the nazis," she says.

Eighteen Maple Trees •

Also in that chapbook were poems about some of the U.P. men I had grown up knowing. My oldest Ishpeming friend, Susan, and I often talk about men. Our picture of the ideal man has to include the working class component—men have to be handy. If a man can't fix things, we feel quite strange. Susan is married to Don, a former industrial arts teacher who can fix and build anything, and both my father and husband were excellent with tools and in building things. What's a man for, if he can't change a flat tire, we U.P. girls were taught to think.

This isn't as crazy—or as sexist—as it sounds. It's a matter of social class. I used to visit my friend Marianne in Hancock, whose father was the head of our branch of the Lutheran Church, at Suomi College. At dinner, I used to be amazed. This man, Dr. Wargelin, sat at the head of the table and conducted discussions about world events. His three children and his wife responded with what they had read in the newspapers or heard on the radio. At our family dinner table I would never have brought up a world event to discuss, nor even a book I had read or an interesting teacher I had.

At family special occasion dinners, with the lace tablecloth out, we would listen to family stories, told by my Aunt Lynn, a teacher to whom I later dedicated my doctoral dissertation. Later, after dessert, we would often sing around the piano. No one ever discussed world events at the table, though once, at election time, I remember being in bed upstairs unable to sleep because of my uncles arguing about whether to vote for Eisenhower or Stevenson, with my father shouting he would always vote democratic because of Roosevelt who brought in the unions, and my other uncles yelling Ike had won the war for us, and so what more did he want? But that is the extent of discussion of world or national events in our household. Later, in Bowling Green, I loved the discussion around my friend Maribeth's, a lawyer's, table—world events, politics, art, music, film.

I heard many discussions about fixing things, building things, running things. The men would talk for a long time about mechanical things, hunting, fishing, sports. My father and a partner ran a decorative iron works welding business. They made many wrought iron fences and railings. Building and making and fixing—that's what men talked about and did.

• *A Writing Life*

IRON WORKER
—to Dean

just spent three weeks
in North Dakota welding
on a power plant
got laid off there too
we drove all night

everyone was at camp
out on the Escanaba
they were surprised
to see me back to the U.P.
so soon and I just couldn't
stop holding her, never
thought I'd have a daughter,
I just carried her around
for three hours, right on
my hip just like a gun

out east, Connecticut
Delaware one of them
me and Jimmie, remember him?
graduated a year behind us?
1960? and Peanuts? he's got
five kids now, we'll drive
out east and work
'til they lay us off

we build enough weeks
to get unemployment
through spring then
start over, we go down
the union hall, they

tell us where there's
work, we take off

don't never want to move
there, though, all the
crime in them cities
got to figure out a way
so we don't have to
60% unemployment,
it's pretty tough to

• *Iron Worker*

Postcard from a Negaunee bar
IRON MINER

had ten years seniority
that's nothin'. though
you'd think if you work
for a company ten years

started with Cleveland Cliffs
after I quit Northern,
not cut out
to be a college student,
liked to party too much

anyway maybe I shoulda'
stayed and graduated,
then I wouldn't maybe be
well, who knows? they're
layin' off teachers too

I quit school and the
money in the mines was good,
you know? worked the Republic
then the Empire, my kids
go to Central in Negaunee
one's in gifted classes,
can you believe that? and
his dad a college dropout

they say the mines'll
never come back, just on
6 months, off 6 months
the price of foreign steel's

too cheap, you know? when
I see someone in a
Datsun, Toyota, Subaru,
some people even have
nerve enough to buy them
up here, don't know
where their bread's buttered

why I just want to smash
that car. Buy union.
Buy American, I always say.
course that's not counting
Canadian beer, want another?

• Iron Miner

BLUEBERRIES

we crouch then sit
so profuse the tiny berries
two-handed we pick
pluck soft-fingered
in this patch on moss
that one under cedar
farther off the path
by rock with lichens
we wander and don't speak
much but we hear chickadees
and the wind soft and august
blue smudged by fingers
plops into the pail then falls
soundless and it fills

WILD RASPBERRIES

nothing so fragile
as wild raspberries
the globules separate
at merest touch
fall into the hand
in sun in a patch
on the largest gem
in the world
Jasper Knob in Ishpeming
near the Cambrian shield
spread in long grass
white pines white birches

she says that's why
I like it here so well
you just go out
to run the dog
get waylaid by raspberries
every trip ends up
with treasure

SAUNA

our feet in buckets we sit
on the top bench in a row
the little kids sit
near the floor

mother throws *löyly*
on with the ladle
steam rushes from the rocks.
we sting.
we put noses in washcloths.
we talk and sweat.

the urgency takes
over our thumping hearts
we run out barefoot
leap in a group
prance down the hill
through raspberry thorn

dive stumble on pebbles
flail in splashes
the water receives us
our shouts and whoops
force us to relief
to skin eskimo warm

we glow in perfect awareness
cool, we climb the hill
to the sauna again
soap up wash each other's backs
run in lather to the lake
and back again this time

this time for the real steam
and back to our holy lake
then pop rolls cold cuts
the ritual of our ancestors
ruddy and calm

• Sauna

REUNION

we see the child
in each other's faces
the flint/glint beneath
20 years of layers

our eyes erase
fat from bellies
stoop from shoulders
lines and wrinkles

we reincarnate
hair and muscles
rock and roll innocents
our pain lines disappear
like forgiveness

we say "I'd know you
anywhere you haven't changed
a bit."
it is the truth.

MUSHROOMS

pine birch spruce
sand ancient-laid
geologists know
the century.
which will be poisonous?
Hiroshima, Nagasaki
dense pack peacekeepers
we collect
consult 3 books.
finally we eat
the puffballs
dry vapor settles
on our tongues
but we know
we will not die
of these a sharp stab
or instant paralysis
delirium coma fever
vomiting retching
we fear the amanita
coy beckoners dead
pretty as plaques
on kitchen walls
elves sit under them
113 varieties
not poisonous
17 carry death
we open a can
of mushrooms later
nothing looks like its photograph

CANOE

cinnamon
water nutmeg
clear
slopes of clay
and pine
with pebble beds
for steel
head

a fly fisherman
becomes an island.

the water
sounds a protest.

canoe
slides and so
keeps the flow
silent

drake mallards
marshall
sportsmen's art print
effigies wild
turkeys gobble
in the brush

the woodpecker
ticks his echo
tock on dead wood

kingfishers swoop

the beavers
girdle griddle
last year's trees

the river
only
sounds
when it hits
an obstacle

in the middle
there is
just
silent
flow

• Canoe

During the early 1980s, I also began answering advertisements for positions in school administration from the Sunday New York *Times*. One of the positions advertised was the principalship of the Hunter College Elementary School, a laboratory school for children with high IQs, connected with Hunter College, a City University of New York institution in the borough of Manhattan. From my dissertation research, I vaguely remembered that the Hunter College High School had been a high school for girls, and in my application I stressed my background and experience in gifted and talented education, as well as my women's studies interests and teaching. I interviewed for the position in the summer of 1983, and it was offered to me. I had a large rummage sale, and dismantled a four-bedroom house where we had lived for nine years. My son Steven was a sophomore in college, studying for his Bachelor of Fine Arts in visual arts from Bowling Green, and my daughter Denise was entering her freshman year in high school. She was planning to spend that year with her father at nearby Port Clinton, Ohio. I was fancy free and ready to see the world. I moved to New York City after all those years of New York City dreaming.

The Hunter College Elementary School principalship is a prestigious position, I came to learn. The school is located on the Upper East Side, at 94th Street and Park Avenue, and it is tuition-free. The pressures of urban life and the state of the public schools in New York City contribute to its cachet. I learned that I could pick up a telephone and talk to almost anyone in Manhattan, including an editor of the New York *Times* or the Assemblywoman who is now the Borough President, in order to get a homeless family with a child in our school out of the Roberto Clemente shelter and into an apartment. The week we were working on getting them out, I had a chance to talk for two hours with Dith Pron, New York *Times* photographer of *Killing Fields* fame while we waited for the dad to show up. We shared our rural backgrounds. Such encounters with famous people were common.

During my five years there, I learned that famous people are just as scared as nonfamous people when the principal calls about their child's behavior. I learned to administer a bus system with nine lines that ran from Battery Park to Washington Heights.

A Writing Life •

I even had my own off-street parking on the school playground, and even though the students sat on my car and ate lunch, or used my car as a backstop for ball games, I didn't care; the privilege of parking off the street for free was the point, not the dents and scratches the kids made. Most importantly for the writing and teaching that was to follow in my career, I learned what high-IQ children are really like—fast, abstract thinkers, precocious learners. Denise joined me in New York City for a year, and attended the "Fame" school, La Guardia High School, studying saxophone, before returning to Ohio, where you can get a driver's license at the age of sixteen, instead of New York City's age of eighteen. I was very sad to see her leave, but what can a divorced parent do when the child has both parents who love her, and an amicable arrangement? The child can move back and forth with ease.

Nevertheless, New York City had its compensations for a single (now childless) woman. I had several friends who also were writing. My friend and neighbor, Sara, a newspaper editor in Bay Ridge, Brooklyn, where I lived, and I had long talks about life, love, our careers, and our kids, during a weekly dinner date after work. Lucia read and critiqued my novel and short stories. When she won the prestigious Iowa Short Fiction contest, we all celebrated. Rena and I discussed scholarly writing and she critiqued my studies and papers (as she still does). Clark, a poet and speechwriter, and I discussed country music, history, and New York City politics. Michael, a mystery writer, came to one of my poetry readings and we fantasized writing a blockbuster novel together called *Blizzard*. Norman, a poet and friend of Tom Waits, helped with my young poets' group and taught me about jazz. Ken, a playwright, poet, and novelist, told me stories about the theater in the sixties, when his play was nominated for a Pulitzer. Writers who were parents at the Hunter School—Marshall, Carl, Nora, Nancy—gave me advice on my writing and showed my work to others. I was in "proximity" as the social psychologists studying creativity call it. (Though not one of these big city connections resulted in a publication, it was fun. My midwest network has been far more productive as far as help.) Good friends! The theater! The movies! The opera! The wonderful food! I wrote many poems, one of them this one.

•A Writing Life

I'M A NEW YORKER NOW

I have 3 keys to my house.
I'm a New Yorker now
I must get locks
for my gas tank, ignition,
hood, and an alarm
on my fender. My antenna
slides in, locks, also.
My insurance is $1600.00.
I don't meet people's eyes
and smile as we pass
I see fearsome creeps
on the subway and don't blink
I drive 10 mph average
on my way to work.
gridlock's a new word I know
I beep swerve
can make a 3 lane street
4 or even 5 lanes

I'm a New Yorker now
can hail a cab
carry many keys
and little cash
few credit cards
walk tough
spread my valuables
about my body
wear low heels
sneakers with my suits

drink soda not pop
wait on line not in line
with great patience
I never knew I had
such patience
I barely murmur
when my bank takes
5 days to clear
a cashier's check

I doubled my salary
1/3'ed my life style
pay the highest taxes
in the country
for roads full of
potholes streets full of filth
schools the middle
class doesn't attend

I'm a New Yorker now
saw Paul Newman
on the street
Sean Connery,
Carl Bernstein
bought me a drink
at Elaine's

I o.d. on possibility
For entertainment I can go
to the opera, the theatre,
a lecture, a concert
museums shops restaurants
neighborhoods bars clubs games

• *I'm A New Yorker Now*

parks walks zoos readings
such riches
no human could possibly
do it all

I'm a New Yorker now
stay behind locked doors
read the paper
watch tv think about it.

My novel, *The Three-Week Trance Diet*, won the Carpenter Press Tenth Anniversary First Novel Contest, over about seventy other entries. Carpenter had several judges who judged the manuscripts anonymously, and the book won by a fraction of a point. It was published early in 1986, with a copyright of 1985. When my copy arrived at the office, I couldn't contain myself. I screamed, jumped up and down with joy. A Buddhist monk who was visiting the school giving an assembly on a run around the world for peace that was to take place asked, "Can I touch you?" He thought I would bring his writing efforts good luck. I hope I did.

I immediately began writing another novel, *The Arrest*. The Ohio Arts Council appointed me chair of its literature panel, and I flew back to Ohio for three years for the panel meetings, seeing my friends in Ohio and staying in touch with the writing community. I continued to write poems and short stories, some of which were published. A short story manuscript was a finalist in the Iowa Short Fiction contest one year. Some of the short stories are finally being collected here. I'm glad they're not homeless anymore.

I also began a nonfiction book, called *Principal*, about being the principal of a high-pressure, multiracial, high-quality urban school with free tuition. The novel and the nonfiction book remain unpublished, though the novel has been nominated for the Pushcart Publisher's Award and it has been a finalist in several contests, and the nonfiction book was sent to Hollywood by a friend who thought Jane Fonda's people might be interested in the urban principal angle. Can you imagine that? I can't. She wasn't. One of my coworkers, the other principal, Alan, said if Jane Fonda was going to play me, he wanted Dustin Hoffman to play him. We missed our chance at stardom, though some of the children in my young poets' writing group and I did make an appearance in a *Nova* show called "Child's Play," about prodigies. The producers called the school wanting to talk to our chess prodigies, and I told him I thought there were writing prodigies also, and told him about my young poets' group. The producers rented a room in the Metropolitan Museum of Art for us to write in, and we walked in and out of the museum several times while they filmed us. We thought we were on our way to our own series. They edited it so that you only get a short glimpse of us at the end of the show. So much for television fame.

I got to travel: the U.S. State Department asked me to consult with American schools in the Near East and Southern Asia. I went to Pakistan, Greece, India, Egypt, and Bangladesh for six weeks, talking about writing, doing writing workshops with the students, and consulting about the education of the gifted and talented. In Islamabad, the wife of the U.S. AID attache invited me to a reception of Pakistani poets who write in English. Several of them also write in Urdu. They gave me their books and we had a fine afternoon talking and sharing poems and stories. Travelling alone in the Moslem world led to several adventures about which I later wrote poems and essays.

That same year I was approached by a group called Reunion of Sisters with a joint grant with the nation of Finland, to be one of the Finnish-American women on the literature panel and on the education panel. My mother and I traveled to Finland with this group in the summer of 1987, where I learned about the Finnish education system and the Finnish literary system. One of my poems, "Grandma You Used To," was translated into Finnish and performed. I was interviewed by the *Helsingin Sanomat*, the largest newspaper in the country, on how to educate bright girls. Later, I wrote an essay and a poem about our search for my mother's grandmother and about being interviewed.

Here is the several times-published grandma poem. I wrote it one afternoon after I just got an urge to pull off the road into a rest area. Call it intuition if you will. I later found out my grandmother had died that same afternoon, at my mother's house in Ishpeming. People seem to remember this and "The Company" the most of all my poems. "I remember your grandma poem," people say to me. "It reminded me of my grandma." The poem seems to have a life of its own. Following it is a Finnish translation of the poem, and following that, a poem about the newspaper interview in Helsinki. They were written ten years apart, but have the same theme.

GRANDMA, YOU USED TO

keep a boarding house you fed pulp cutters
and ore dock men and railroaders up at 5
each morning packing lunch buckets
changed their beds fed them dinner too
for three bucks a week *work work work*
you yelled to my mother and aunt at dawn
sleeping behind the draped arch front room
(now my mother feeds you baby food)

       Grandma you came over
on the boat to the promised land in '07
from finland to be a maid in the U.P., Michigan
they beat you your cousin took you away
to the next town you were 19 you cleaned up
after rich people; *work work work*
you yelled at my grandfather a handsome lad
dark wavy hair who drank 'til you
divorced him when people didn't get divorced
(now my mother changes you)

       Grandma you scrubbed
floors at the hospital a scouring maid
dumb finn crabby lady on your hands
and knees a cow a garden and four kids
can't even talk english waiting on people
all your life; *work work work*
you yelled at your grandchildren whose mother
was having a baby on your hands
and knees scrubbing clean floors
(now my mother spongebathes you)

• Grandma, You Used To

                              Grandma your mother
wouldn't marry your father in Finland
she was a weaver travelled then town to town
with you the fatherless child the outcast
laughed at and scorned so when I came to you
pregnant with my new young husband you held
my hand on your knee and said love each other
in a language I never learned: *rakastakaa*
before you died you wanted to make for
my mother serve her just one cup of coffee

    That poem was translated into Finnish and published in 1993, in an anthology called *Juuret Suomessa,* honoring Finland's seventy-fifth anniversary of independence. It was translated by Auli Talvi, and this is how it reads.

MUMMU SINULLA OLI TAPANA

pitää poorititaloa syötit metsureita
kaivosmiehiä rautatietyöläisiä ylös viideltä
joka aamu eväitä pakkaamaan
laitoit vuoteet syötit päivälliset
kolmella taalalla viikossa töihin töihin töihin
huusit äidille ja tädille aamutuimaan
nukkuivat verhon takana kadunpuolella
(nyt äiti syöttää sinulle vauvanruokaa)

Mummu sinä tulit tänne

laivalla luvattuun maahan 07
Suomesta piiaksi ylä-Michiganiin
sait selkään serkkusi vei sinut pois
naapurikylään olit 16 siivosit
rikkaiden jälkiä töihin töihin töihin
karjuit isoisälle komea mies
tunna kihara tukka ryyppäsi kunnes
otit eron silloin kun ei vielä erottu
(nyt äiti vaihtaa sinua kuiviin)

Mummu sinä hinkkasit

sairaalan lattioita kuuraava piika
tyhmä äkäinen suomalaisakka kontallaan
polvillaan lehmä puutarha neljä lasta
ei puhu englantia palvelemassa
kaiken ikäsi töihin töihin töihin
huusit lapsenlapsille joiden äiti
synnytti lasta konttasit
polvillasi hinkkasit lattiat
(nyt äiti pyyhkii sinut sienellä

Mummu Sinulla Oli Tapana

Mummu sinun äitisi

ei mennyt vihille Suomessa
oli kutoja kulki kylästä kylään
mukanaan sinut isätön hyljitty lapsi
naurun ja pilkan kohde kun tulin luoksesi
raskaana nuoren miehen kanssa otit
käteni polvelle sanoit rakastakaa toisianne
kielellä jota en oppinut: rakastakaa
ennen kuin kuolit halusit sovitusta
äidilleni tarjota hänelle kupillisen kahvia

Mummu Sinulla Oli Tapana •

I'M IN THE
HELSINGIN SANOMAT

I'm in the largest newspaper in the country
they even took a picture
**"Lahjakas tyttö tarvitsee
erikoiskannustusta"**
How should bright girls be educated?
They called me "Rehtori"—Headmistress.

Last week we unearthed the truth.
My mother and I found her grandmother
Anna Kärnä of Vimpeli in Ostrobothnia
a maid, mother of an illegitimate daughter
my grandma Ida who immigrated to the U.S.

we finally found you Great-grandma Anna Kärnä
in an unmarked grave
up in Lappajärvi in the churchyard
Grandma you used to
is my poem about Ida, your daughter
you never saw again
it's been published all over the place
Finnish-Americans like me to read it out loud

Great-grandma I was born on December 19, too
Great-grandma you used to
live in potato fields near a large lake
work at a store
be an unmarried woman with shame
Great-grandma was my great grandfather
the boss's son?
we looked for him, too, but no luck

• *Helsingin Sanomat*

boss's sons like to lie with maids

Great-grandma you went to a round
yellow church by a quiet river
we bought you a headstone in the grave
lent you by relatives or neighbors—
we don't know which—

it says *Äiti* ("Mother")

Great-grandma you eventually
became grandmother
to four U.S. grandchildren
eleven great grandchildren
seventeen great-great grandchildren
and more coming

They interviewed me in the *Helsingin Sanomat*
about how a country like Finland
should educate its bright girls
I say, *"It's an old story. Send them in shame,*
 (humbled and poor/ yearning to breathe free)
on a crowded boat to Ellis Island in the U.S.
Teach them to work hard
keep cows and a boarding house
four children and a drunken husband
overcome poverty in the second generation,
send the next generation to the public schools
send their children to the state universities
and this third generation will come back
and you will treat them like experts
interview them and ask them questions
as if they aren't really
the great-grandchildren of peasants"

Helsingin Sanomat •

That poem is a summary of a larger essay, collected here. I was amazed that I would be thought worthy of a story in a Finnish newspaper. When I asked myself why, I came to the conclusion that since my family had come from the lower classes in Finland, and my grandmother was illegitimate, I thought I would be viewed as not worth interviewing. My other grandparents, the Piirto side, my grandfather Herman Piirto, and my grandmother Sophie Vähäkorpi, also seemed rather poor and dirt-scrabble, when we visited their birthplaces in the Ilmajoki area. Otherwise, why would they have emigrated?

Yet we as children were taught to almost revere anything Finnish all the while our elders were trying to be as American as apple pie, to out-American the Americans. Some of our aunts and uncles even felt ashamed that they hadn't spoken English when they went to school, and they were quite touchy about supposed slights because of their ethnicity. Altogether, it led to a mixed message about being Finnish-American.

When I lived in New York, I was invited by the Finnish Consul General's office to a few parties, at their elegant apartment on Fifth Avenue overlooking Central Park, and I read some poetry at a do at the New York Public Library sponsored by the Finnish consulate, and I got to meet real Finns in sumptuous settings. That was also odd to me, as I had the picture from my childhood of Finns as old ladies who spoke Finnish and knitted, cooked, and shuffled along slowly down the aisles after church in their black overcoats and black hats.

I often used to drive my Ishpeming grandmother, my Piirto grandmother (the "Grandma, You Used To" poem is about my Marquette grandmother, my Eskelinen grandmother) and her childhood best friend, Mrs. Ruusi, to church. The two women had arrived together as girls to Ishpeming from Finland and they spent their adult lives living two blocks from each other. They used to call each other every day to check in. I remember them talking in Finnish with great earnestness. Recently I received a wonderful letter from Jack Ruusi describing his grandmother, how she would wind her long gray hair into a bun, how she would be constantly knitting socks, mittens, sweaters, or crocheting bedspreads or tablecloths, how she would cook him hearty meals and how devout she was. The sophisticated Finnish diplomats I met in New York were not like our Finnish grandparents, to say the least.

Recently I went to the Finnish service at the Bethel Lutheran Church. The pastor was in his early sixties, of the second generation, and the Finnish rolled off his tongue with great shudders of r's, poundings of k's and t's, and melodious accents upon the first syllables. The congregation was also of the second generation, and they seemed very respectful. At the earlier English language service, not one of the men had a suit on, unless you count the guy in the 1970s aqua leisure suit, but here, all seven of the men had formal dark suits on, with white shirts and ties. Likewise, the women were dressed up. At the earlier service in English, few of the women looked so well-groomed; the garb was casual, sweaters, pants, down jackets. Here were dresses and jewelry.

The music of the liturgy was familiar, and my mother and I found the words in the hymnal and sang along. Finnish language singing at Suomi College taught me to sight read the syllables. The hymns had many verses. My aunts recall that my grandmother knew all the verses by heart. I used to come down to get my Grandma Piirto in the church basement, and all her friends would shake my soft young hand with their knobby, translucent, hard, dry ones that had known much hard work. Sometimes I'd arrive early, and have "lunch," coffee with sugar cubes, date bars, coffee bread, prune tarts. There is still a coffee hour in that same church basement every Sunday, between services.

It seems duller and shabbier now, and sometimes I sit there drinking my coffee while my mother chats with her friends. I look around that church basement and remember all those old Finnish women, chatting away under bright lights, eating on china plates that the church used to own. The piano was by the wall in front, and they would sing long songs and be joyfully exhorted by the pastor. Then the sliding serving window would open and the women who had to serve would display the delicacies for the *kahvi* hour. Our mothers would say, "I have to serve in church today"—

meaning one had to go early, stay late, unload the food from cake and bar transporters (usually Tupperware), put it out on serving plates, make the coffee in the large pots, wash the dishes and clean up afterwards. All the food was home-made. If a woman brought store-bought delicacies, she would feel a little ashamed.

During the Centennial year of Ishpeming, 1954, the women of the Bethel Lutheran Church, the Bethel Guild, made a cookbook. Some of the receipes featured hamburger, mushroom soup, and jello, as the second generation tried to be more American than the Americans. This cookbook, written by our mothers, the contemporaries of the people so conscientiously attending the Finnish service in 1994, also featured such delicacies as *lettuja*, thin Finnish pancakes, eight kinds of rye bread as well as that old staple, cardamom bread. There were also saffron bread and pasty (indicating the influence of the Cousin Jacks from Cornwall on the local cuisine), "kala loota," [note: spelling is as in the cookbook] a fish and potato dish, herring salad, "kalvisijilta" (Swedish jellied veal), "juustoa" (Finnish cheese), "pannukakko" (oven pancake), and "kulta-vellia" (fruit sauce). It contained Finnish pecan balls, Swedish tea rings, and white Spry cake. It contained receipes for using blueberries—pudding, cake, sauce—but no recipe for that Christmas Eve treat we kids hated, that foul-smelling fish soup, "lipia kala," of cod soaked in lye. Perhaps our parents thought that soup was so entrenched in the culture it didn't need to reach immortality in a church cookbook.

The old ladies (and a few old men) at the Thursday night Finnish service didn't care about acting American—most of them never learned English—but they certainly wanted their children to assimilate. The grandparents would line up for lunch and keep on talking in Finnish. I want to say the cliché, "chattering brightly," that is used to describe cocktail parties. The room *was* bright, friendly, warm, welcoming. All the ladies are dead now, and their elderly children attend the Finnish service once a month, where church is special and one dresses up. Here is the essay, "The Search for Anna Kärnä" that I wrote in 1987 after the Reunion of Sisters trip to Finland with my mother.

THE SEARCH FOR ANNA KÄRNÄ:
An Essay

It had stopped drizzling. We wheeled the rented VW Golf into the small town, our first view the view of the river, and then, behind the trees, of the church. My mother pulled out the Christmas card she had carried here, from half the world away. It was a black and white photo of this very church, in a yellow cardboard holder, photographed from across the river at a site we couldn't pick out now. She had taken the card from her mother's effects when cleaning up after her mother died. Parking the car in a side road in one of the few available spots, my mother asked a man rushing with the rest of the people, why all the traffic, and where was everyone going? "National baseball tournaments," he said.

Baseball? In Finland? Here, in Ostrobothnia, in a small small town on the shores of a lake called Lappajärvi? Had we come around the world to a baseball tournament? Our curiosity piqued, we resisted the temptation to follow the crowds, and went toward the church instead. The date on its stone gateposts said it was 150 years old, and the metal gates were held by a large iron clasp that we lifted. The gates slowly swung open and we entered the church yard. The bell tower rose above us, the yellow clapboard siding newly painted, the cross on top of it pointing straight.

We began to look at gravestones, looking for the name of her maternal grandmother and my great-grandmother, Anna Kärnä. All four of my grandparents came from Finland, which means that all eight, sixteen, thirty-two, of my great-grandparents did, as they had for my mother. My children are only half-Finnish. When I got married, my aunt said, "But he's French. Your children will be half-breeds." The quiet of the walled-in churchyard seemed paradoxically medieval, as we heard the echoed bellow of the announcer from the field.

My mother said, "She said she lived across from the church," as our search ended. No people with those names who had the right dates. This, our first cemetery, did not yield the information we wanted. But what information did we want? To find the burial place of our ancestors? To find living relatives? To get a sense of where our people had come from? To touch our pre-conscious past? All of these and perhaps more.

As we crossed the street, my mother read the name on that Christmas card that had been sent to my grandmother so many years ago, from a friend in this village, Vimpeli, where my mother's mother, Ida Kärnä, had grown up. I saw two women emerge from the house across the street, and said to my mother, "Perhaps they know. That house is across from the church." My mother opened the painted white gate, walked the path next to the clotheslines, and greeted the women. "Do you know any Peltolas?" she asked. The lead woman looked at the card, looked at the name, and said, "Yes, sure. She lives just over there. Let me take you."

We followed her, and my mother chatted in Finnish with her, telling her we had come to try to find some information about her mother's mother. A block away, we entered a small garden apartment in what looked to be old folks housing; at least there were the old men sitting outside on the bench, and a small and institutional feeling to the apartment. My mother knocked, and an old woman, dishevelled and disoriented from the nap we had interrupted, answered. We entered, and our guide asked Mrs. Peltola whether she had sent the card. She looked at it, puzzled, and then admitted it was her handwriting, but she couldn't remember sending it, nor could she remember to whom she had sent it. My mother and her sister and two brothers had been the children of two Finnish immigrants who had come to the United States and had settled, met, and married in the Upper Peninsula of Michigan, in the second decade of the twentieth century. My aunt Tyne was born in 1915, my mother in 1916, and my uncles Arvo and George in 1917 and 1919. Their mother, Ida Kärnä, my grandmother, had never talked about her parents, except for a few references to her mother.

Strangely, my mother and her siblings had not bothered to ask, sensing my grandmother's reluctance to discuss her past and the reasons she had immigrated. Finally, when my grandmother was in her eighties, my mother had asked her the hard questions that had been troubling her, and my grandmother said that she had been illegitimate, but that she occasionally saw her father, Antti Santala, when she was growing up, remembering that he had played horseyback with her on his knee. My

• The Search for Anna Kärnä

grandmother gave no more information, except that my mother always knew in the way that children know things, that my grandmother loved her mother dearly. By now, what had happened here in Finland in the nineteenth century, perhaps a furtive night between a young couple of different social classes, the maid and the master, has produced four children, eleven great-grandchildren and fourteen great-great grandchildren, with the latter now reaching childbearing age.

And now my mother, over seventy, had come to Finland with me for the first time in her life . We were attending a conference to be held in Helsinki and at the University of Kuopio, called "Reunion of Sisters," where 300 Finnish women and Finnish-American women were to meet and talk. I was on the Literature Task Force, since I write fiction and poems, and I was to present a paper on Finnish-American women writers. One of my writer friends said, "You and who else?" "Well," I said to him, "Jean Untinen Auel is one of us. You know her *Clan of the Cave Bear* and *The Mammoth Hunters*?" I was also to perform the "Grandma You Used To" poem at one of the evening events with an actress reading the Finnish translation .

What a great chance for my mother, a widow who lives in Ishpeming, Michigan, and who had never been to Europe, to come along. What a great chance for us to travel together. My mother has spoken Finnish all her life, and has been studying how to read and write the language for the last few years in a night class taught by a Finnish immigrant. Finnish has thirteen cases and many endings, and words get added to each other, so that one can have a word with as many as fifty letters. My knowledge of Finnish is odd words, for food mostly, and I know that Finnish words are all pronounced with the accent on the first syllable—HELsinki, and SAUna. That's "sow" as in female pig, or as in "ouch," and not "sow" as in apposition to "reap." Besides the sauna, the Finnish immigrants' other contribution to U.S. culture was the co-op apartment, the first ones having been built in Sunset Park in Brooklyn, in "Finntown." Even though I attended Suomi College, the only Finnish American college in the U.S., I was so stupid at the age of seventeen that I didn't even avail myself of the opportunity to study the language of my ancestors, a regret I continue to have as I am pulled into the Finnish-American community by friends and people who share their stories with me.

As soon as we got off the plane and rented the car, my mother was one-minded. Go to the Christmas card's small northern town, Vimpeli. We had spent the night in Tampere, a clean textile manufacturing city with cobblestones and flower boxes, and this was the afternoon of our second day, managing the European sign language and the Finnish language road signs with many laughs and wrong turns. The roads in Finland are very well-kept, as is everything there, and the countryside most closely resembles the Upper Peninsula of Michigan, or the upper regions of Wisconsin and Minnesota. Lots of lakes, forests, fields. It is no mystery why the Finnish immigrants settled along the northern tier of the U.S. and in Canada. Only about 300,000 Finns emigrated to America, and about 55,000 of them returned. The census of 1980 showed about 600,000 Americans claiming Finnish ancestry.

In 1990 I was reading poetry in Little Rock, Arkansas, and I met a woman from Massachusetts who was half Italian and half Finnish. She said seeing my name and hearing me read my poetry infused with my Finnishness made her weep for the invisible half of her, the forgotten half of her that hadn't been recognized in immigration history, though a Finnish immigrant is supposed to have been the first president of the U.S., before Washington. And now, here we were, in Vimpeli, after eighty years, trying to find traces of an immigrant peasant girl, her mother, and her illegitimate father.

Mrs. Peltola couldn't remember, but she had probably known our grandmother while growing up, even though she is younger. "No matter," our friendly guide, whose name was Kirsten, said. "We'll make some calls. Come over to my house and have some coffee." So we trudged after her back to her house, and entered. Our second Finnish house. Like the first, there was no grime even in the corners of the entrance porch, but just a rag rug, and shoes on the floor. We didn't know whether to take our shoes off as we entered, or whether the pile of shoes was only for members of the family, so we left them on. Kirsten showed us into the living room, through the large dining room. The dining room table we passed was piled with fabric. Curtains. She is a custom designer of curtains, and the other woman who now greeted us was her employee.

The other woman, whose name was the same as my mother's, Helmi, was less effervescent, reticent. They cleared the curtains they had been folding into curtain boxes, off the table, and my mother stayed in the dining room, chatting, while I sat down in the living room and looked around. This was the second time in the last half-hour I had felt like a little girl again, with the ladies talking in Finnish, and me unable to understand them, as had happened so many times in my girlhood. The living room had a TV, a VCR, easy chairs, some original paintings on

• *The Search for Anna Kärnä*

the walls, momentos of trips, African dolls, a plaster statue of Venus de Milo about two feet high stood improbably near the wide entranceway. A TV guide in Finnish on the floor. Photographs of two young men about seventeen in what looked to be yachting captain sailor caps, but which turned out to be graduation hats. I recalled similar hats in Bergman movies.

Most times when you enter someone's home you don't have time to look around, unless you're a child who must be silent. I had the time because I was like a child, tongue-tied. The poet Aili Jarvenpaa has a poem about how her children can still recall every detail of the pillows in her mother's living room, how the crocheted patterns went, because her children had been made to sit while the Finn-talk went around them. When Aili read that poem, I recalled my own very vivid memories of my grandmother's living room--her gloxinias in the planter, the satin, fringed pillow from Okinawa that Uncle George sent during World War II, the pink sugar mints she had in a covered green Depression glass dish, the doilies over the backs of the chairs, the mottled wine and green vines on the area rug.

And of course the African violets. My grandmother was one of those people whose African violets always bloomed. I was to find out that all the Finnish homes we entered had success with African violets. Kirsten's were set in just the right light, with several shades of violet and pink peeping out from the green velvet leaves. Now, in my late forties, I am finally having success with African violets, and so I have a theory that African violets only bloom for middle-aged and older women. I have a corollary that when our African violets bloom for us, we begin the middle-aged stage of our spiritual journey, and often go back to the church. My mother had never seen her grandmother's African violets. My mother had grown up without the comfort of a grandmother. I had known both my Finnish grandmothers, felt their substance in their hugs. Someone of that generation of grandmotherless immigrants said she always cried when they had to sing that song, "Over the river and through the woods, to grandmother's house we go."

The call that *kahvi* was ready came, and I entered the dining room, where Kirsten had effortlessly whipped out a feast--Karelian pies, heated through; scented cardamom *pulla* coffee bread, cold cuts and cheese layered in a circle on a glass plate; sliced tomatoes and cucumbers; small cookies with almond flavoring; thin-sliced dark rye bread; and the coffee in demitasse cups with a choice of *kerma* or *maito*, real thick cream or milk. Every restaurant we went into offered real cream for coffee. Memories came to me again, of all the coffee tables I had sat around with my aunts and grandmothers. Particularly vivid is when my aunt was divorcing my uncle. All the aunts sat around the dining room table on Saturday nights and Sunday afternoons, in rooms similar to this one, drinking coffee and dissecting the relationship, always agreeing that he was a rotten guy to give up such a good woman as our aunt.

My cousins and sister did the same thing for me when I got divorced, and I left feeling better, also. Sometimes it is difficult to separate these times from those; women sitting around a table, with the nieces right in there with them, talking about men. One of the residues of my Finnishness that I retain is rushing to offer coffee to any visitor, however unanticipated, at my house. During my childhood, many people, on Sunday afternoons, used to go "visiting," arriving unexpectedly at friends' and relatives' houses, to great welcomes and good *kahvi* talk. The invention of the television has probably isolated us. I remember the visiting stopped about the time that Sunday afternoon football started, during the late 1950s in our town.

While I surveyed the living room, Kirsten had made a few quick calls, trying to find the minister of the church, so we could get a look at the records, but everyone was at the baseball game, she said. I said I wouldn't mind going to see the baseball game; I had never even heard of Finns playing baseball until this very minute. And here was the national tournament. We all agreed it would be fun to go over to the baseball game. Helmi left for home, her day's work over. Helmi tied her *huivi* or scarf, on backwards, where Kirsten tied hers under her chin. A conscious class difference? We shook hands with Helmi and thanked her—-*kiitos*—-as we parted on the street, while Kirsten hung a few clothes on the clothesline before we left.

Kirsten's husband, Kaarlo, and their two sons were at the game. We got to the field and Kirsten collared the English teacher from the local comprehensive high school to talk with me and explain the game. It was the last inning. Nine innings. But there are five outs in Finnish baseball, and no pitcher. Or the pitcher doesn't pitch; he throws the baseball up in front of the batter, from the side of the batter, and the batter slams it out into the field. There are many fielders, and if the batter hits a good one--what is "good" escaped me, for many times a ball would be a good bouncer out to center field, and it would not be counted fair, or it would be a long pop fly and be caught and look like an out, but the batter would run--towards third base. Or maybe I was watching a game in reverse. Then the batter ran across the middle of the diamond towards first base, and then to second, third, and finally home, in a very confusing zig-zag.

The English teacher couldn't tell me much more than what I was seeing with my own amazed eyes, because he wasn't a baseball buff nor had he played when he was a kid, and had only been to three games that entire year. He said the rules had always confused him, too. His English, spoken in a British accent, was excellent. The game ended, with Vimpeli losing the national championships to a town just north of Helsinki, and most of the crowd left with sad faces. A sad day in Mudville. The players on both teams looked like baseball players, all right, stocky, muscular, handsome, not long and lanky like basketball players, nor massive like football players. As in most of the world, in Finland, football is soccer, and Football is called "American Football." The players all looked like my son. In fact, one of the most striking impressions of being in Finland was how everyone looked like me.

Used to the diversity of urban U.S., I was struck by the sameness of faces as is every traveller who goes to any mono-ethnic, monochromatic country. During the entire time there, we saw about five blacks, ten Indians, and four Asians. Students, or travellers, surely. Finland has a very conservative immigration policy, and an even more conservative refugee policy. Thus, one of the most curious sights was that of the ladies in long black full skirts with aprons and vests and lace-edged caps, whom we saw all over, pushing baby carriages and shopping in the markets, speaking fluent Finnish. I thought these were Bohemian immigrants, but after I asked I found that these are gypsies. At the market in Helsinki, there was a gypsy lady selling very beautiful lace and crocheted tablecloths. We did not see any gypsy women with booths at any of the other markets we visited, though. Someone told me the Finns still discriminate against gypsies, and that there has been a settlement, or reservation, made for them up near Lapland.

After the game, we were invited to stay with Kirsten and Kaarlo, in one of the bedrooms upstairs. At dusk, about 10:00 in this northern latitude in August, we drove out with them to their cabin by the lake. Again, this was like the cottages many from the Upper Peninsula have on northern lakes, except it was more Finnish in decor, of course. Kaarlo had built it all himself; as we entered we gasped. It looked like a picture in an Eero Saarinen or Alvar Aalto coffee table book. Light, varnished wooden floors and panelling shown off by red and white rag loomed carpets running along the floor; a free-standing staircase to the loft in the same gleaming wood; a huge fireplace of stone. Immaculate, of course. Outside, the outhouse, and the sauna, just like at home in the Upper Peninsula.

A truck drove up. "This is a Kärnä," they said. They had called the Kärnäs they knew, and a young man of about thirty had come to meet us. He and my mother talked a little about what we knew about her grandmother's brothers and sisters, since all Kärnäs are supposed to be related, and they all decided that we would have to wait until morning, when we could get to the church to see the records. "And then," the young Kärnä said, "if there's nothing there, we'll take you to The Island." There is a Kärnä Island on Lake Lappajärvi. I pictured us rowing over in the billowing fog in a silent rowboat to "The Island" to find our ancestral place.

Back at their house, Kirsten had heated the sauna for us in case we wanted to take one. They seemed a little surprised at our ease with saunas. The sauna was in the basement, and Kirsten gave us towels, and pointed out the shower, the faucet for filling the buckets from which we would splash *löylyä*, cool water from dippers, onto the rocks, and left us. The sauna was not hot enough, as they probably thought we could not stand it hot, but we didn't say anything. We came upstairs with wet hair plastered to our skulls, just like at home, and we went into the living room, where they showed us videotapes of their son's wedding, with the traditional community folk dance that lasted two hours, with accordions and drums and throwing of the parents and the couple up into the air, with stuffing into pockets of money.

My mother woke me up with her gentle voice: "It's 10:30 and I've been over to the church and I've found things out." She had been up at six, as usual, jet lag not having hit her as it had me, and had coffee downstairs with our hosts before they headed across the yard to their curtain shop. My mother had been introduced to the *Pappi*, or minister of the big old yellow wooden church across the street. He had gone into the records, and had come up with this information: Anna Kärnä had given birth to Ida Kärnä, my grandmother, my mother's mother, in 1890. Anna was born in 1854, on December 19, the same day as I was born over eighty years later, in Lappajärvi. December 19. My birthday. I had been born on the same day as my great grandmother, almost a century later. Anna Kärnä had been a *piika*, or maid, at the time of giving birth. Ida had left for the U.S. in 1910, at the age of twenty. Anna had been buried

• The Search for Anna Kärnä

in Lappajärvi, in a family plot, in July, 1933.

Taking awhile to absorb this information, I calculated, and with amazement, said, "Mother, she was 36 when she gave birth to Grandma!" Thirty-six in 1890 must have been very old, especially in a farming community in rural Finland. "The mystery deepens,"I said. My mother didn't appreciate my humor much, but she asked me whether I thought I was Nancy Drew or Jessica. "Look, Mother, she got knocked up by some guy from town, playing with the maid. It's very obvious to me." I was being deliberately crude, to put some reality into this romantic search. My mother repeated the story her mother had told her about her father playing horseyback with her on his foot with her clinging to his knee and she told me to watch my language and have some respect.

"And he visited once in awhile," I continued. That's the story. Grandma was shamed and felt out of place, and that's why she came to America. Being in this small town, you can see how she would want to come." And then my mother told me that her mother had said her father, Antti Santala, had wanted to put her in his will, because she was his first child, but Grandma had been proud and refused. Now all this information was coming out slowly, in dribbles. It's what intimacy does. My mother and I had not spent so long a time together alone ever, as in a marriage before the children come, and the details were unfolding.

"We go to Lappajärvi," she said. Lappajärvi, when we consulted our map, is just around the large lake, not far, about 30 kilometers. Before we left, we said our good-byes to the sons, who had come to say their own good-byes. Kirsten gave us linen towels with "Vimpeli" woven into them, as gifts when we parted. I gave them a copy of my novel, and my mother gave them some American scented soap from a Prange's department store branch in the Upper Peninsula. Before driving out of town, we stopped to enter the church Grandma had attended, which was festooned with flowers, because a funeral was going to take place. We sat quietly, reverently, and we imagined a young girl here at the turn of the century, sitting in one of these pews, listening to sermons and choirs as the daughter of a maid, a maid herself. Grandma had also worked at a store, my mother then recalled. The old, weathered building across the street was the old store, *kauppa*, and we circled it with our cameras and our imaginations, peeking into the boarded up windows, imagining Grandma there selling buttons and nails and coffee.

As we drove around the lake, we talked of how Anna Kärnä and Ida Kärnä, must have taken this very road before it was paved, and seen these shores, with these reeds' ancestors, these farms with their cows situated in picturesque postures. Cows never look anything but picturesque. We were in a companionable dream, seeing these familiar yet ancient woods, the sunny light making all seem indelible and incandescent. And what about that mysterious "Antti Santala"? Who had our grandfather been? When we drove into Lappajärvi, we asked directions to the church, which, again, like many of the churches in Finland, is situated on a hill near the water, with the graveyard around it. This church was also yellow, with a bell tower stuck with the little statue of a man asking for alms for paupers. It was founded in 1737, and was celebrating its 250th anniversary, signs told my mother.

A cursory search of the graveyard and no Anna Kärnäs, though there were Kärnäs. No Santalas, though there were Santalas in the Vimpeli graveyard. The act of conception must have happened in Vimpeli. We entered the church, and I signed the guest book. There were three teenagers there, and I asked if anyone could speak English. "Yes," a girl said, in perfect American. She was an AFS student from Cleveland, and this was her hostess and her hostess' boyfriend. The boyfriend said the minister was on vacation and couldn't be reached, the church office was in the government building (Finland's church is a state church), and that if we would wait a half hour while he practiced, he would try to find the assistant minister for us. He practiced, and we sat, in the church with stressed-glass opaque windows. The church in Vimpeli had plain-paned windows so you could see the trees outside waving and moving. We sat on firm, old, light wooden pews, and he made the magnificent pipe organ talk, the sound bouncing off and echoing back. Bach.

We followed him along the unpaved roads of the back neighborhoods of Lappajärvi, to the assistant minister's house. The assistant minister was at the Rest Home. To the Rest Home. The assistant minister said he didn't know anything about the graves and he knew the name Kärnä, but not Santala. Reino would know. Who is Reino? The head gravedigger. The young organist called up Reino, and Reino said he would meet us at the church. He peddled up on his bicycle, and shook our hands with a firm grip, the odor of last night's *koskenkorva* on his person. Reino was in his 70's, like my mother. I wondered whether she would like to be fixed up with Reino. I liked him. He was solid and firm, like the miners in my home town. She told him our problem.

He took us to all the Kärnä graves, shook his head at Santalas, and nothing was Anna Kärnä. "1933?" he said. He took us down the slanted path to the end of the second-to-last row by the shore of the lake, and pointed. "Here. It must be one of these. These are around that time, July, 1933." There were two small mossed-over pointed stones on two graves. No names. Paupers' graves. The graves of dead single poor women. I snapped a picture. My mother was silent. She wanted to check the church records. "Come back Monday," Reino said. "The church office will be open. I will meet you here at the graveyard at noon." It was Friday. What would we do until then? My mother and he talked a little more, and she mentioned one of the names of Anna Kärnä's brothers, which she had written down when she talked to her mother. "Adam?" Reino said. "Adam Kärnä? Sure. I knew Adam Kärnä." Adam lived over on the island, and had a big farm. His children were called something else, people changed their names, and married, and all. Mother wrote down names, and to the island we went.

There is only a small, about twenty-foot bridge, to the island. No rowboat necessary. We entered the Finnish kingdom of Kärnä. And followed our first directions from Reino. We wound around on a woods road past farms. Lost. We asked a man unloading his pickup truck. Over there, across the main road. We went over to the main road and across it, winding down a long hill. The place we were looking for was "white," and "near the lake." No road led to the lake, that we could see. We turned left, dead end. Up again. Saw some kids on dirt bikes. Mother went out to talk to them. They said, a yellow house, over there and down that road. We asked them to lead us. Followed the kids on the dirt bike. Went to the lady outside hanging her wash. Over there, she said. I took pictures. Down the road. Into a blueberry forest. Woman picking blueberries with a cunning blueberry picker that scoops the berries with tongs, then puts them into a container with a flap. She pointed down the road. We turned in. Wrong farm. An old man said, "It's the farm up there, right next to the road, but he's probably not there, now, staying at his children's in town, may be back at night." She knocked at the door. He wasn't there. Mother tried another name she had.

By this time we were very confused, with all the names and the changes, and wondered what we were doing here, with not even a clear purpose for this search. Why were we searching for Anna Kärnä? Over the main road and up, said the woman with the 2-year-old clinging to her skirts as she picked potatoes. Down the road. An old woman who looked like my Grandma Ida Kärnä Eskelinen, was walking down the road in her *huivi*, her sturdy shoes, safety pins pinned to her dress. I flashed a memory of seeing Grandma walking down Third Street in Marquette, about a mile from home, in her late seventies, while I was in college at Northern. I stopped and said,"Grandma! Mummu! Do you want a ride?" And she laughed at me for even offering such a thing, and talked about how healthy walking is, and scolded me in Finnish. She said I should walk more and not always be in a car. We stopped and asked this lookalike about the names, and gave her a ride to the end of the road. Up there, she pointed. Laughing. We knew we were the best excitement to come to Kärnä Island today, and that people would be calling each other up and talking about those *amerikan-suomalaiset*. She knew the name, Antti Santala. Was a schoolteacher, she said.

    One ranch house, brick, in potato fields. A young woman, blond children behind her, staring, said her husband's grandfather would know, at the house around the corner of the road. She said she'd call him while we headed up there. Mother's command of the language was, of course, necessary, in order for us to be even having this adventure. Though most students study some English, older people don't know any, and the students are very shy about speaking. If I had undertaken this search for our roots in these potato fields, I would have been lost a few blueberry patches, cow pastures, and dirt bikes ago.

    But I was good for something. I can drive a stick shift like nobody's business. Spraying dust on the tracked road, we approached the farm. The house was butted right against the road. I stayed in the car while my mother talked to the old gentleman who came out to greet us. As I sat, I noticed lilac bushes, apple trees, the vegetation familiar to me at home in the Upper Peninsula. A cat played in the gravel with a butterfly, tumbling. I wondered how my whiny Siamese cat was doing back in Brooklyn, being looked after by my Greek-immigrant landlady.

    A woman in jeans paused to look at me from the barn side door. She disappeared. Soon she reappeared, in a blue coat like a doctor's coat, a scarf tied around the back of her head. Getting ready to milk the cows. We found out later, at the conference, that Australia has many Finnish immigrants, and when the agricultural representative came to Finland, seeking to get farmers to come to Australia, his last question, after all the willingness from the families to emigrate, was a question to the men, "Are you willing to milk cows?" he would ask. Most of the men would answer an emphatic "No," but if a man would hesitantly say, "Yo," the Australian government would invite the family to emigrate. Milking is women's work in Finland. When my grandmothers came to America,

• The Search for Anna Kärnä

they changed that custom, and my father and uncles milked.

A man came across the yard with a load of sticks probably for a fire, in his arms. Then my mother gestured for me to come in. I entered a large room with a tile furnace at one end, a sink, a stove, a picnic table in the middle, long runners of rag rugs, a tv, two huge rocking chairs in front of the tv. McLuhan was right: it is a global village. Television is everywhere. That spring, even in Islamabad, in Dhaka, in Karachi I noticed that video stores were all over, too. The summer of 1990, in Argentina, the televisions were blaring the news of the World Cup Soccer victories in Italy to Buenos Aires, where I stood on the pavement outside the tv stores with the crowds, shouting at the Argentine hero, Diego Maradona. CNN is the channel of choice all over the world. Maybe Buckminster Fuller was right, too, that the world will be saved not by governments, but by young businessmen with attache cases and pin-striped suits, making agreements to promote international commerce. Or cinema.

This room, like others we would see, had many woven wall hangings, *täkänäs*, " and hooked rugs, *ryijys*, and photographs on the wall. In order to check whether these people in this functional farm house might be our relatives, we went back into the unused living room. They consulted the family Bible, and pointed to a *ryijy* on the wall that had woven into it, the family lineage. No luck. No mutual recognitions. More names were mentioned, and the old man had a memory of who our people might be. He called them up on the phone. Yes, said the person on the other end. Come on over. The old man said he would come with us and show us the way if I promised to drive him back.

We arrived at another farm, a few hills and dales, potato fields and fertilely cultivated lands away, over dirt roads. A lot of cows. Out came a man called Väinö, who resembled my Uncle Arvo. It turned out, it was true; he is my mother's second cousin twice removed, as we figured it. In the farmyard were the same boys who had led us on their dirt bike to another farm. They were his grandsons, our cousins, too. Väinö pointed to his son's house just about fifty yards away, across the farm yard. He invited us, and the old man, in. Coffee was served. The wife hovered, washed dishes, served, smiled in friendship, and only at my invitation, sat down with us. The two men and my mother talked Finnish.

I and the wife didn't say anything. I thought the conversation was going swimmingly. I heard the word *sukua* a lot, which, by this time, I knew, means "relative." I thought I was actually following the conversation, though I couldn't open up my mouth to speak a word of Finnish. But I wasn't following it all that well, because later, my mother told me that the old man and Väinö had to be brought back to the topic often, as they really wanted to visit about milk yields and not dead relatives. Did they have any photos? my mother wanted to know. Väinö cursorily searched, and then said, no, someone must have taken the family album. He gave us more names, including one of a cousin a few miles away. Väinö gave us what was to be our only description of a living person's memory of Anna Kärnä. Väinö said he had met Anna Kärnä once, when he was eleven, when she was visiting her sister, his aunt. "She was small, like you," Väinö told my mother, "and very, very quiet."

    The old man was restive and wanted us to bring him back home. I said to my mother to tell them we were going to go to Seinäjoki for the night. "Seinäjoki?" said our cousin Väinö. "That's too far. Stay here." I didn't think the invitation was sincere, and my mother hesitated, and went along with me. Later, in talking about it, we thought his reticence might have been that notorious Finnish reserve, and we might actually have been rude in not staying there at the dairy farm. But how were we to know, being more American than Finnish by now? In the early 1990s, there was a segment on the television show *60 Minutes* about the Finns and the tango, showing how the Finns have adopted the tango passionately (or as passionately as such non-emotive types can show) and how they line up to take tango lessons or to go to tango parlors. Tangos were played by young Finnish folk-artists on tour in the United States at a concert we attended. I thought I was in Argentina. That *60 Minutes* show also had a telling—and touching—moment where a modern young Finnish woman said that when sophisticated and urbane Finns play at flirting, they say "I love you" to each other—in English. But when they revert to Finnish—*mina sinu rakastaa*—"I love you" really means what it means and is not casually taken.

    Not knowing what to do, or whether the invitation was serious we said we had an appointment on Monday at the church with Reino, figuring that if Väinö wanted to see more of us, he would be able to find us through Reino. We drove the old man back to his house, headed back to town, and down the 50 or so kilometers to Seinäjoki. We were hungry, even after all that *kahvia*, perhaps from nervousness and excitement, and we tried to get a table in a quiet spot of the place. We got a table in the back, but the music was Madonna's newest hit, loud. As we ate our local fish dinner (very good), we discussed our search. We wondered who

Antti Santala had been. Had he been the younger man toying with the maid? A travelling schoolteacher, such as they had in those days? An old friend? A rogue? Had Anna gotten pregnant in Lappajärvi, and then come to Vimpeli to be the maid and to have her baby away from the tongues and eyes of her friends and relatives in her hometown?

Had Antti treated her with respect? Was it a one-night stand? My mother recalled the story her mother had told her about seeing her father while she was younger, so at least our great-grandfather was around afterwards. So it must have been impossible for him to marry her. My mother was more kind than I in discussing the morals of the man, wanting to give him the benefit of the doubt. I wanted to make him a heartless rogue, or as in a Finnish folk song we knew, a *hulivili poika*, a wild boy, sowing his wild oats. My rakish great-grandfather.

Saturday morning in Seinäjoki. We had in mind to spend the weekend searching for my father's side of the family, but were hesitant how to proceed. We didn't even know what we were trying to find. So we went shopping. Across the street, the Sokos chain department store. Soon my mother got lost in the book section, laboriously translating titles. I found a book about Finland in English, and read the whole thing while my mother performed her concentrated and oblivious dawdling that has amused and frustrated our family all our lives.

I was reminded that Finland has fought four wars since independence, in 1917, and they had over seventy years as an independent country, that the wars had been devastating, that hundreds of thousands of young men had died, and I remembered the two cemeteries we had visited, with their special sections for war dead, row after row of young men with the same birth year and death year. I read about World War I, and the Winter War in the late 1930's with Russia, and about the German retreat from Norway down through Finnish Lapland during World War II. I remembered a picture book, at my aunt's house, in Finnish words I couldn't understand, with brown photographs of men in white suits on skis, sniping Russians from behind trees when the men came out to pee in the morning. I remembered the last movement of Sibelius' Fifth Symphony, with those soaring octaves that somehow move me to tears, which Sibelius composed during the last battles of World War I. Mannerheim's name was mentioned a lot. As many men had died as those of our grandparents who had emigrated earlier in the century. All disappeared from the country of about four million, two generations decimated, significant in such a population. Many of those who emigrated earlier in the century, left after refusing conscription into the Russian army. Finns for a long time called those who emigrated, cowards, deserting the homeland when things were tough, and it is only recently that they have begun to feel friendly to the emigrants. The author said that Finland has the fastest-growing economy in Europe, and proudly recounted that Finland is about the only country that repaid its war debt to the United States.

An hour or so later, my mother was ready to really shop, and we went upstairs to the domestics section, and bought linens and towels and tablecloths for gifts. The Iitala glass section, the Arabia china section, the Marimekko linens section, all available in America, beckoned us, as well as the Aarika wooden jewelry, the local brands. Finland is very expensive, and we felt it as we spent our marks in ethnic pride in the beautiful Finnish designer merchandise. Someone later told us that the Finns aren't such good designers now they've gotten comfortable.

Monday and back at noon in Lappajärvi. No Reino. We had spent a happy morning on the road from Vasa, the city on the Gulf of Bothnia with much Swedish influence, eating sweet peas and throwing the shells merrily out the window, sucking on strawberries we had bought from the market square. We felt a little forlorn as we walked the graveyard of the yellow church on the bluff by the lake, searching again for Anna Kärnä. No Reino and what were we to do? The church secretary. I remembered the way, and drove there. By now it was 1 P.M., and we went into the municipal building.

Upstairs, my mother talked with the secretary, who said she didn't have much time; she was alone here trying to answer the phone as well as take care of city records, and everyone was on vacation. Besides, she was about to get off now. I said in my best savvy New York voice, "Pay her and I'll bet she'll find the information." My mother said we would have to come back tomorrow. Tomorrow? And where would we stay? The secretary said there were no hotels or motels in the area, but there was a campground with cabins. We followed her directions and arrived there. I was ill-humored, and my mother was disappointed. Another day in looking at graveyards and searching for what. Would we ever find Anna Kärnä? We were lucky that someone was there at the campground. Though we didn't realize it, for it was only August 17, the season had ended. Children were beginning school this week. Families had ended their vacations.

We were shown a cabin that cost 200 marks, cheap for Finland.

• *The Search for Anna Kärnä*

It had a fireplace, a sauna, a front porch with water to look out on over the distance, a little kitchen, and two bedrooms. We took it, and went up to town, about eight kilometers away, and bought some food at the local supermarket. My mother got delayed at the bread, and then at the dry cereal, reading the ingredients on the labels, for she belongs to the natural food co-op in Ishpeming, and I gagged as I passed the blood sausage with memories of my father's penchant for it, settling on some Karelian pies, some cold cuts and some cheese. The new potatoes looked good, so we took some of those. Cucumbers. Tomatoes. Some fake wine that when I drank it, gave me the worst headache I have ever had. Liquor, wine, and full-strength beer are sold only in government stores. Drunk-driving laws in Finland are so strict that there are hardly any alcohol-related accidents.

Back at the cabins, my mother said we should try to find the other cousin Cousin Väinö had mentioned. My mother didn't seem to want to go back and visit Cousin Väinö at his dairy farm. My mother had asked the church secretary where she lived. Her name was Aila Koivisto. So we drove again, searching for "a gray house just by the side of the road, you can't miss it." As before, we took the wrong road, ending up on a logging road in the woods. When we finally found the right road, we went right past the house because it didn't look like a house; it looked like a weathered barn. When we finally knocked on the door, unannounced, we were invited in by a woman who looked older than she was. Aila Koivisto never married, and worked for years in a nearby town in a factory until the factory closed. Now 59, she had come back to the Lappajärvi/Kärnä area where she had been born. Both parents had died, and she had only a few distant cousins with whom she didn't socialize, because she was not as well off as they. She lived in her parents' *tupa* or "cottage by the lake," though it was really about a quarter mile from the lake and right on the road, as described.

Inside, Aila lived in one room that contained a wood stove, a table, a narrow bed, a sewing machine with a doily, some chests, a sink, a refrigerator, and the omnipresent African violets, doing very well, thank you. She offered us *kahvia* and for the *pulla* took out some frozen rye bread and rolls which she thawed in the oven. The freezer was full. She had attended a concert two nights before, a choir from Sudbury, Canada, from the Finnish Lutheran church. My first and only trip to Finland had been as a member of the Suomi College Choir, in the summer of 1963, when we had toured all of Finland as the official choir of the Lutheran World Federation which was held in Helsinki that year.

My mother and Aila talked and I assumed my role as the silent daughter, speechless observer. Aila had a beautiful thick bun on the back of her head, grey with streaks of blond. Her hair must have been long and beautiful, archetypically blonde and Scandinavian, and in fact, when people had described her to my mother, they had said "Aila has a big bun on her head." When she moved, she moved with litheness and a female grace that would be provocative, and probably had been. Single, childless, sexy. A survivor in a nation where her whole generation of men had been slaughtered. A factory worker retired and now living out her life on her country's democratic socialist pension in a small drafty house in a small rural town, going to church and to choir concerts on her bicycle, or on the bus.

Aila pulled out an old photo album. My mother was asking everyone we met for a chance to see old photographs, hungry for a glimpse of her grandmother. There were none of Anna Kärnä, though there were many of Liisa, Aila's mother, Anna Kärnä's niece, when she had been a servant girl in Manhattan for eleven years until she had come back home for a visit, met Aila's father, and fallen in love. Aila's mother, though she knew English, had not taught Aila, but had come back and seamlessly reassumed her rural ways. Immigrant girls all sent photographs back home of themselves attired in fashionable hats and dresses, urban magazine plates, as if to tell the people back home how well they were doing in the new land. This album was full of such photographs, of Liisa and her friends. Liisa had worked on the Upper East Side of Manhattan, a few blocks from the school where I was a principal.

So Anna continued to remain a mystery to us. As we drove back to the cabin, we were silent, thinking about our cousins and their lives here in Lappajärvi. That evening, we wandered the paths near our cabin. No blueberries. The lake. A sauna. Postcards. A fire in the fireplace. Early to bed. Early to rise in order to get to the church office on time.

I decided to walk, and my mother took the car up there. My walk along the lake and the road with my notebook, and the wildflowers the same as back home in the U.P.—foxglove, Queen Anne's lace, chicory, goldenrod, and those strange gray crows—brought peace. I felt at home here. A cow in the meadow mooed at me. The way the carpenters lapped wood on the barns was similar to barns still standing in the immigrants' new homeland in the Upper Peninsula, a pattern brought over and made part of my visual understanding how barns should be built, just as were the patterns in the sweaters and mittens we saw being knit by women standing in the markets, similar to those my grandmothers had knit. The crafts of the immigrants' hands lived longer than they did. And Anna Kärnä lived only in the fleeting memory of Väinö when he was an eleven year old boy.

Up at the church office, my mother had the information. Anna Kärnä had, indeed, been buried in this cemetery in July, 1933. In a family plot. She also had the names of forebears for another century or two, though it was very difficult to read the ones dating back to the early 1600's. We went back up to the church again and walked the paths, searching. Finally we came to that row where Reino had pointed out the two small pointed stones on two graves in 1933, and my mother resignedly took a picture of the stones. This must be her grave, all right.

"I've been thinking," my mother said to me, as we sat sweating in the sauna, throwing water on the rocks. We've always had important talks in the sauna, and this was to be one: I could tell by the tone of her voice. "I think we should buy Grandma a headstone. It's a disgrace that she doesn't even have a headstone." I sat silently, and knew that this was probably the reason for her being so impelled. Something was telling her to come and make things right. Grandma Anna Kärnä was sending her a message. Come to Finland and validate that she had lived and died and given birth to some Americans.

"I agree," I said. "Let's do it. How much does a headstone cost? I've got American Express, if they'll take it. I've got enough room on my Visa, too." We went to bed and slept a good sleep. After breakfast, hot chocolate and cheese, my mother told me what she had been thinking of in her dreams. She wanted to make sure that one of those graves was in fact Anna Kärnä's, so we would go and get Aila, because Aila knows the ways of the town. Then we would go up to the church office again, and find out the number of the grave plot. When we arrived on Aila's doorstep at 9:30 A.M., Aila didn't even look surprised. She said to give her a few minutes to change clothes, and she would be glad to come with us. Aila and my mother went up to the church office. They came down, and said they had called Reino, and they had the exact number of the plot: 192.

Reino came bicycling up, and we began to walk down the paths of the church yard. It was a cold and blustery morning and we were shivering in the wind. Reino didn't know which one was 192, so he went into the church. A few minutes later, two handsome young men arrived wearing rubber boots. The city engineers had been on the premises. They had with them a large scroll, and as I peeked over their shoulders, I saw them pointing to 192. Then we all trooped behind them, to the opposite side of the cemetery from the 1933 paupers and single women's graves we had thought was our grandmother's. Next to a thick, short stone wall, beneath a birch tree, there was a pause in the lineup of headstones. "There." The man pointed. "There." In a family plot. But not of Kärnäs, Koivistos or Rautalahtis. Of Hytinens. No one we had met had even referred to Hytinens as relatives. I thought of the Hytinens I had known growing up in Ishpeming, Michigan. Were they my cousins?

    We had found Anna Kärnä's grave. The yellowed scroll of the map of the church even had her name written there. I saw it. "Anna Kärnä." It was unmarked. No one had bought her a stone. And so we did. Reino said he would do it, and he wrote down the words we had thought to put on it. *"Äiti"* (Mother). *"Anna Kärnä." "December 19, 1854 - July 15, 1933."* We went to the bank and bought a cashier's check and put the check in Reino's hands. Aila said she would get hold of a camera and take a picture of it. We were free to go. My mother's search, my search, was over. The picture arrived a few months later, along with Aila's Christmas card. We plan to go back, to find Antti, that wild and irresponsible great-grandfather who played horseyback with my grandmother on his foot, kicking her all the way to Michigan.

. . .

I left New York City in 1988 and took a job as a professor of gifted and talented education at Ashland University in Ashland, Ohio. My fellow principal's and my services were no longer wanted. The uproar and the trauma that followed the announcement of our leaving and the necessity to face it with a minimum of emotion and even—*Sisu*—has left a permanent scar. I still haven't stepped foot over the threshold of that Upper East Side address. My friend says he is still repressing the experience; though we both went on to better jobs, the public nature of the deed stayed with me in the form of shame. Here is when writing as autotherapy helped. The winter of 1988 I wrote everyday, documenting daily life in a school, in *Principal*, the nonfiction book. The situation gave the book drama. Writing it perhaps saved my sanity.

When I got this job I still have in Ohio, my old stomping grounds, I came back to my original profession, college teaching. My writing continued; I always write poems, for myself, for friends, and I submit to the occasional journal that asks me. Life in this quiet college town has helped me publish two long nonfiction books, *Understanding Those Who Create*, with Ohio Psychology Press in 1992, and a textbook called *Talented Children and Adults*, with Macmillan in 1994. I won't talk much about my scholarly writing here; just know that it is grueling, difficult, and detailed. For the Macmillan book I had an acquisition editor, a production editor, a copy editor, an art editor, a photo editor, a marketing manager, and their various assistants calling me and asking me things. I had to obtain permissions and releases. I had to read, understand, and summarize many books and articles. I was very tired when it was all over. I did those two books in three years, and I am proud that I was able to do that. Don't ever put down a person who writes a textbook. It is very hard work and requires a lot of stamina. Such work also requires creativity, discipline, and constant thought. The writer is often obsessed with the current book, article, or study and haunts the library, the computer database, the bookstore shelves, the scholarly journals, for the latest thought and interpretation in order to assimilate it into the total picture, to synthesize and analyze in order to explain, to show a bit of truth.

In 1990, I applied for and was given a Fulbright-Hays study grant to Argentina. My project was to write a cycle of poems, and

I did so. A manuscript of my travel poems to Argentina and to the Near East and Southern Asia won an Individual Artist Fellowship of $5,000 from the Ohio Arts Council in 1993.

But let me talk about what it means to travel, to see what places look and feel like. As a writer, I can imagine almost everything but place. I was glad to see what the Himalayas and the Andes looked like. Now I can use them as setting if I wish. I wrote a screenplay about the Afghan War when I took a screenwriting class. It is called "Mujahadeen." The first ten minutes were almost entirely visual, with only two words—"It's done"—as I moved my main character (a teacher, of course) from the "R" train on 59th Street in Brooklyn, to downtown Brooklyn, to Kennedy Airport, to Islamabad, and to Peshawar. I couldn't have done that if I didn't know the places. Likewise, the only full-length play I've written, called "Tornado," uses tornado country as its setting. I couldn't have written it if I hadn't lived in and on the prairies where tornados come whipping through every spring. Thus, place is also important to the imagination as ground, as set.

The writer Winifred Gallagher in her book, *The Power of Place,* described many environments that humans are attracted to and posed questions as to the reasons we choose places. Perhaps my attraction to the location in Ishpeming is as simple as its strong magnetic force, with all that high-powered iron there. She said the mystery of place for artists may stem from the combination of early emotion and association with pleasure and play as well as strong family and community ties. Gallagher said that cues from the environment stabilize or destabilize us and so we go back to places which helped us. As I noted in *Understanding Those Who Create*, like dogs circling, or athletes putting on the same socks for each game, rituals in these places help us recapture the feeling that gets us into what the psychologist Csikszentmihalyi calls "flow," the state of mind necessary to write or create. "Flow" is the sort of energetic, electric, modified trance state that one experiences when one just *knows* there's a poem there. I myself am inspired and prefer to write in the Upper Peninsula, but I can write anywhere. Here are poems written in two different faraway places—Buenos Aires, Argentina and Skardu, in northern Pakistan in the Himalayas.

Postcard from Skardu, near Afghanistan

EASTER

flew up here
next to peaks of Himalaya
25,000 feet high
poked above flurries of clouds
eye level with K-2
the highest mountain
in the world this year

woke to bright blue sky
thin above etched peaks
with chickadee cousins
calling, hopping in apricot
blossoms at 6 a.m. on Easter

trout kiss the pond surface
reflecting stony foothills
across, villagers slowly climb
their walled paths to work.
Sunday is no holiday for Islam.
hungry herds of goats bleat

a cock crows more than thrice
the sound almost as perfect here
as in Epidaurus' amphitheatre.
a bee begins to sing

yesterday dusty laughing
begging children chanted
"1 rupees!" following me
swinging their arms
to imitate my western gait.

stern older brothers
forced their sisters' heads aside.
girls cannot be photographed
without their veils.
they look at me as if I'm naked.

today the tribal waiter
asks me whether I will
fast for Christ.
I tell him his valley
choirs my sunrise service

sing him a verse of
He Lives! He Lives!
and that old song
the men's choir
at Bethel Lutheran Church
used to sing each year
Up from the grave He arose

everywhere the sound
of rushing water.

• Easter

Postcard from the Plaza de Mayo

EVERYWHERE THE VOICES OF THE MOTHERS

the mothers, fathers, daughters,
sons all have explanations

"my skin got goosebumps
when I heard the names"

"the *subversivos* called my grandfather
the same day they bombed his best friend"

"he left the country
because they threatened
to kidnap his children"

"he said, 'come and get me,' defiant,
and they did, they put a bomb in his car"

"we sent our children away
 to a relative in Italy.
they were in a high school drama club
they never had an armband in their hands"

everywhere a story

"the *subversivos*, those communists
started it right here in Cordoba
go to the corner and see where
they massacred the people"

"intellectual college professors,

can you imagine? like the Shining Path
in Peru. Leftism gone too far."

"I'm glad the military took over
but they went too far."

"I saw priests
mowed down in my church."

"the Mothers are all communists"

"all the disappeared showed up
in Sweden and the United States.
I used to play soccer with them."
"they took my daughter-in-law
and my son in the middle of the night
and stole their furniture too"
"my daughter went crazy in jail"

every Thursday at four, mothers
the conscience of the world
the Mothers of the disappeared
no matter who they were or why
march at the Plaza de Mayo
Argentina says the women will die soon
"they are getting old"
all the people say
Nunca Mas — *"Nevermore"*
and Presidente Menem
pardons the colonels

• Everywhere the Voices of the Mothers

Another thing that happened when I moved to Ashland was I went back to the Lutheran church. For several years, I had attended workshops through the Omega Institute and the Open Center in New York, continuing my search for spiritual wholeness. I felt a real spiritual yearning after the collapse of my job in New York City, and when I attended the Trinity Lutheran Church on Center Street here, I found myself weeping at the songs and at the liturgy. The relief I felt in having found a job—a good job, my ideal job, a tenure-track college teaching position, and the release of the pressures of trying to hold up my head in public for the kids, teachers, and parents, came together at church, and I just thanked God and wept. For some reason, my sense of being back with the tradition in which I had been raised gave me joy. I joined the choir and sang in a women's trio.

I had left the church as a cynical intellectual in the early 1970s, and neither of my children was confirmed, though they were baptized. But I rejoined the spiritual, traditional home where I had spent my youth. The landing has often been rocky and I often have grave doubt. My problems are still those of making that Kierkegaardian leap—merely those of committing faith, belief, and trust in the context of my normal state of intellectuality and skepticism. But that's another autobiography. The connection between the spiritual and the creative is a deep one.

As we age, they say we get more concerned with ultimate meanings, and become much like we were during the pure searches of our mid-teens. My quiet life as a professor and writer, with my kids grown and gone to their adult lives (my daughter Denise, her husband Ralph and my son Steven live far away and they are happy and we have raised them well), my continued constant reading, my interminable wondering, have fostered the thoughts written down here in this essay, during this year of my life, and at this place where I live now.

How is intuition formed? One teacher at a dream workshop I attended pointed out what should have been obvious to me—that intuition and inspiration have to do with natural breath. How does an artist know what to make art of? To write of? Why is place so important in this intuiting, this knowing? Why am I yearning to write every time I am in the Upper Peninsula? After all, I haven't been able to live there for over twenty years. Perhaps my natural breath is freer and deeper there.

Perhaps this essay and poems give some insight. Recently I flew on a commuter plane to Houghton from Detroit, over the clear cut forests and deep open mine pits. I scrawled notes in my notebook. I took pictures out of the plane window. Is it true you have to leave a place in order to see it clearly? I feel no such yearnings to record the scenes and sights of Ashland, Ohio.

In our location, in Ishpeming, there lives a woman I have never met. She has a black Labrador retriever, is fit and looks in her thirties. She wears jogging shoes and a sweatshirt tied about her waist. Every morning she passes my mother's house, on her way to walk her dog in the fields and woods at the end of the street. Often she is walking with a male friend. The dog runs ahead, without a leash. Sometimes I fantasize I am her, at home in our location, with a companion and my dog. I am living in my old neighborhood, or at our camp on Helen Lake, writing, observing, and thinking. There it is different. I am in the woods and the land where I belong, alone yet free, treasuring my solitude yet ready for any adventure.

None of us knows what will happen next. Maybe I will, by some miracle, find a job in the Upper Peninsula that is equal to my job here. But here isn't bad. I have good friends, a good job, and a loving family. We are distant in geography yet always in touch. I have a house, a pen, books, a computer and music. I am healthy and probably getting wiser all the time.

Last Christmas, I sent this last poem to friends and relations from near and from far. I have been sending poems as Christmas cards since my creative writing breakthrough in South Dakota in the early 1970s. Some people now have twenty years of seasonal records of my writing life. Here's 1993's poem and I will close this chapter of my writing life with this meditation. I also sent a photograph of the sunrise described here, and people told me looking at the photograph while reading the poem was quite calming. Imagine you are in this northern place, seeing the red-orange, yellow, blues, blacks and browns of a new dawn. ***Breathe.***

MEDITATION AT HELEN LAKE, MICHIGAN

Smoky vapor off the lake.
Remnants of coals stirred
in the stove in the outdoor fireplace
rekindle in deep ash.
The sun is arriving again.
Leaden pewter clouds lay scattered
across the golden luminescent east.
Above, patches of blue promise a fair day.

The dog Jessie sighs in her sleep
while far-off geese cry at breakfast.
The handle of the cup is cold
but the coffee is warm.
Earlier, rising to light the wood stove,
I heard the crackle of flame begin
with crumpled newspapers and kindling;
then I cuddled back into the drowse
of my warm sleeping bag.

Now, small birds dart in the spruce trees
in front of this primitive porch.
They do not stop long enough
for me to identify them.
The deep pleasure in writing
what I sense overtakes me
here in the morning at the table.

Wild phlox, goldenrod nod in dawn air,
catching the magical red-orange light.
Blowing east, the mist begins to dissipate.

The perfect reflections of clouds
and birch shore laden
with fern, moss, and brush
paint the still still lake surface.
The cabins on the other side slumber,
though one burned a bright beam
in three directions last night
while I swam after sauna in moonlight.
Pure elements:
earth, air, fire, water coalesce.

My mind drifts as is its habit
to my grown children,
gone to their lives but not
from encompassing protection
of loving thought,
and the questions:
now I have finished this textbook
how will I fill time?
now I'm 50
what meaning will life take?
where will the path go next?
in this exquisite natural tranquility
one discovers in middle age
where wisdom is nascent
I wish I knew that bird's name—
Hopper, Flutterer, Splasher in the water.
Such solitude is necessary.
This peace is joy.

THE END

• Meditation at Helen Lake

Here is an essay I wrote about the most famous Upper Peninsula citizens of my home town, Ishpeming, a musical group called Da Yoopers. My town also claims Glenn Seaborg, the atomic scientist, whose father and grandfather worked in the same brownstone shops where my father worked and who even has an element named after him, the element Seaborgian; Kelly Johnson, aeronautical engineer and contributor to the invention of the P-38 Lightning plane, the B-80, F-104, U-2 and other jets; and John Voelker (pseudonym Robert Traver, the author of **Anatomy of a Murde***r) but nowadays, in the Midwest, it is Da Yoopers who take the prize.*

DA YOOPERS DECONSTRUCTED

A few years ago, there rang throughout the airwaves of the clear channels of WJR radio in Detroit, a song called "The Second Week of Deer Camp." This song, about a camp full of flatulent men and lots of empty beer cans but few deer, caused many a smile on the faces of commuters stuck in gray sky November traffic around the Detroit area. I understand the same thing happened in Milwaukee and Chicago. Da Yoopers, the people who sang this song are like I, also natives of Ishpeming, Michigan, and by now may be the most famous—or infamous. The song catapulted them to regional fame. Their concerts are sold out as thousands of people rock and roll to the words of this bar band who started writing their own songs about their own land.

I listen to the tapes of their songs whenever I am nostalgic for the thick accent of the natives of Ishpeming and Negaunee, the central Upper Peninsula of Michigan. There is one man on the tapes who sounds just like my father. He is the man on the "Rusty Chevrolet" song, a song sung to the tune of "Jingle Bells." That accent is something that has been educated right out of me, and I regret it during the times that I listen to Da Yoopers.

When you drive on US 41 past Ishpeming, you see a place called Da Yoopers Tourist Trap. The establishment is recognizable by the figures of the canoeist in the lumberjack flapped hat pulling a water skier in long underwear, and by the pink flamingoes on the front lawn. Parking next to a tableau with deer playing cards and hunters gutted and hung out to drip gut blood into the snow, you go up the ramp and enter the building. A busload of Boy Scouts may be giggling at the first thing you see. These are canned partridge gonads, porcupine peckers, fish assholes, canned fresh air, mugs proclaiming "Rusty Chevrolet," a booklet, "Da Yooperland Dictionary," to read in "Da Yoopers Reading Room," the outhouse. You see bags of Trenary Toast ("dunk it in coffee like a real yooper does"), bottles of maple syrup made in Champion, and tapes and CDs of Da Yoopers songs. So far there are no refrigerated cases of *juustoa* (Finnish cheese) or potato sausage.

"Da Yooperland Dictionary" contains such terms as "pills" as in "I gotta pay da pills"; "raha," or money; "shining" or using lights to poach deer or bear; "mud" or coffee; "no hunting" or this sign should be shot; "Dominic Jacobetti," a state representative of immense power in Michigan; "Carl Pellonpaa," a host on a local Finnish-American television show, *Finland Calling* (and a native of Cleveland Location); "stump jumper" or someone who works in the woods; "swampers," or rubber boots worn in mud; "trash fish," any fish that is not a native brook trout; "troll," someone from downstate, below the Bridge; "youbetcha," a common phrase meaning "yes"; "pasty," a Cornish meat pie, or "Yooper soul food"; and "tanks," an expression of gratitude.

The bathroom humor continues on other shelves throughout the store, with numerous models of outhouses and signs to put up in the outhouse, past sweatshirts proclaiming the U.P. as the land of 10,000 Makis. (The joke here, to those in the know, is that "Maki," a Finnish name as common as "Smith," means "hill," and so the Upper Peninsula is the land of 10,000 hills, as Minnesota is the land of 10,000 lakes. Get it?) Several comedy albums have now been made, all of them proclaiming that people from the Upper Peninsula, or Yoopers, drink a lot of beer, work in the mines or in the woods, pick each other up in bars that play country-western music, and just generally live a happy-go-lucky rural life. Their women are fat and their men are fatter, with huge beer bellies. They drive rusty Chevrolets and get sick of shoveling snow. They play cribbage and horseshoes and make love in the sauna. They are in exile when they have to go "down below" (the Mackinac Bridge) to work. They perform ancient rituals when there is not enough snow, dancing around trees on the lawn and shouting to the snow god, Heikki Lunta.

When deer season comes, everyone takes two weeks off; the men go to camp and play cards, drink, drive around getting lost, and wipe themselves with Sears Roebuck pages. The women become deer widows and go shopping in Green Bay, or go out dancing, picking up deer hunters from down below at the local night spots—one club famous for this purpose was the Diamond Club, now a restaurant. This is a world where everyone has a nickname. They say, "What the hey?" They go to snow machine races, Brewers games, and wake up in fields among cow pies after blackouts from drinking whiskey chased by beers.

They say the reason drinking and driving is bad is that it makes the beer spill. Their older relatives become addicted to Bingo games at the reservation in L'Anse. They love their children and willingly attend two-hour long seventh grade band concerts at the National Mine School. They advertise items for sale on "Buy, Sell, or Trade" on the local radio station, which features a company which makes several sizes of condom—hot dog, bratwurst, and zucchini. They own stinky beagles that ride on the tops of the boxes in the beds of their pick up trucks. They wonder whether they'll be late for work because their cars won't go during snow storms. Even neighbors with four-wheel drive cars get stuck.

The men look like this: they wear Martinen's Gas Plus baseball caps stained with chain saw oil, and have three-days of stubble on their faces. They wear red and black flannel shirts, have beady eyes, red noses, and jeans with the crotch hanging down to the knees because of their big beer guts. They wear swampers and have big feet. They lay on the couch and their wives call them "the couch that burps." The women look like Maki's cow and roll over and crush their husbands while making love. These women eat cudhigi sandwiches (Italian sausage), Tino's pizzas, pasties, and the cookies and blueberry pies they bake. They drink Miller Light. Their husbands love them anyway. They call the Upper Peninsula "the last frontier," where nothing is easy. They split wood, swat horseflies and deer flies and the mosquitoes are true killers. But they thank God they live in the Upper Peninsula, where they don't have to lock the doors, even though they work for minimum wage. They laugh at people exiled below the bridge, who warn "don't go up 'dere" where the U.P. natives still have to carry water from the stream and where the bears will get you.

Da Yoopers Tourist Trap is a "goldmine," a dean in the engineering school at Michigan Tech tells me. He is from Negaunee and is as nostalgic as the rest of us for this mythical land of the U.P. that Da Yoopers proclaim in concerts throughout the Midwest. A dean at Northern Michigan University gave a serious scholarly paper on Da Yoopers at a conference in Chicago where he reported that they gross about a million dollars a year, and are geniuses at self-management and self-promotion of their comedy albums and routines.

This dean, who had been living in the Upper Peninsula for only a year, also said that the first day of hunting season is a "national holiday" in the Upper Peninsula, and that "they" (meaning people who live in the Upper Peninsula) don't do any work during hunting season; even the university professors cut school. When I mentioned this comment to university professor friends they were quite irate. I told the dean my father never owned a deer rifle, and none of our teachers missed school when I was growing up. I said I feared that he, like Da Yoopers, was stereotyping the people of the Upper Peninsula and he apologized. He sort of mangled the pronunciation of the band's last names: "Du-cu-ah" for *"De*Caire " (emphasis on the first syllable) and "Poh-t*ee*-ya" for "*Po*tila " (emphasis on the first syllable). In fact, it's pronounced by natives, "*Poh*-t'la." As in Finland, you seldom go wrong in the Upper Peninsula if you emphasize the first syllable of a person's name, no matter the name's nationality.

One Sunday after church and brunch with my mother, as we idly wander around the tourist trap, I overhear a young couple earnestly discussing a purchase. I transcribe their conversation, pretending to be taking notes about the lace-edged tablecloths. "Get him a can of fish assholes. Do it," says the man.

• *Da Yoopers Deconstructed*

"I don't want to do it. I'll just send him the tapes."
"How about the porcupine peckers?"
"I got him the deer turd necklace."
"What's the difference? A turd necklace or fish assholes?"
"Let's just get him a bumper sticker."

I watch them and they go to the bumper stickers and get him the green and white one that says, "Say ya to da U.P., eh?" Yes. This was an actual conversation overheard at Da Yoopers Tourist Trap, where bathroom plaques proclaim "Bear Bottoms Welcome, But Please Don't Leave This Room UnBearable," and a U.P. weather map says, "Shitty, Pretty Shitty, and Really Shitty" with regard to the weather, where safe sex is a dog jumping on your leg, and Da Yoopers Moose Rut Beer is Brewed in Yooperland USA, Brewed from the U.P.s finest Moose Nuggets. All these are for sale. I used to have that same "Say ya" sticker on my car when I lived in New York City, and someone flagged me down on the Brooklyn Bridge as we were stalled in traffic, and asked me what language my bumper sticker was in, Dutch?

The rest of the store is filled with what my Jewish friends call *Tchotschke*—tourist trap junk mixed in with reprints of nature paintings from local artists, some quite talented, with sculptures of mushrooms and toadstools, Christmas ornaments, sauna soap and sauna towels, His and Hers bathhouse coin banks, carved stumps and birdhouses, mixed in with photographs from the old mining days and samples of ores from the area and from India, China, and South America. They have Michael Loukinen's films of the U.P. culture, "A Good Man in the Woods," "Finnish American Lives," and "Tradition Bearers," and a rack of books pertinent to interest in the area, as well as prominently displayed CDs, cassette tapes, and videos of da reason for all this hoopla, Da Yoopers. Local advertisements said that Da Yoopers are looking for old cars, old snow machines, and other machinery to put into a museum that will be attached to the property.

On a summer evening in August, Da Yoopers give a free concert in town in honor of the Upper Peninsula Volunteer Firemen's Annual Convention being held there. The vacant lot on the corner of First and Pearl Streets, where there used to be a furniture store, a grocery store, and a dress store, fills with people, locals and the firemen. Many fists grip many beer cans.

Da Yoopers take the stage and say they are going to try out their latest album, "One Can Short of a 6-Pack" before they go on an extended tour of county fairs throughout the Midwest. They say that finally they got booked into Duluth by a promoter, and 2500 people showed up in a hall made for 900, so they guess they won't have any trouble playing Duluth in the future. My childhood friend from Cleveland Location, Linda Lou, and I find a spot at a picnic table with five young mothers who have just finished their summer classes at Northern Michigan University and who are celebrating. This is both Linda Lou's and my first Yoopers concert, and as they swing into their familiar comic territory—the snow, deer camp, fishing, hunting, and the relations between the sexes—we clap and hoot along with the rest of the crowd.

Like the rest of the audience, we are glad they have sold a fishing song to Hollywood. We laugh at the clowning and prancing cross-dressers in wigs with balloons for boobs who remind us of the Benny Hill show. Our laughter is a little nervous at times, not as hearty as that of the seventh grade boy standing next to us who can hardly contain his glee at the fart jokes, nor as rousing as that of the beery woman standing up and clapping, her beer can in a toast sign in the air, nor as the man next to us who takes off his t-shirt and flops his flabby belly in time to a song about how men's beer bellies make it difficult for their wives to find their penises.

The leader of the band, Jim DeCaire, thanks his mother who is in the audience, and we all clap. He thanks Tony, a local restaurateur who owns the Venice Bar where the band got its start in 1963. They go into their last song, a song about bum sniffing, where DeCaire, dressed as an old man, puts on a gas mask and nuzzles it into the rear end of the keyboard player, Lynn Coffey, who is dressed as an old woman. Agism and sexism are not concepts Da Yoopers care about, though DeCaire made a public service radio announcement played throughout the Midwest about snowmobile safety after he himself had a snowmobile accident one winter (while partying, the rumor goes). Though Linda Lou and I wince, this is all good naughty fun to them and to most of the audience. DeCaire ends the show by complimenting the firemen on their bellies which were on display during the dress parade earlier in the evening. People flock to buy t-shirts which proclaim, "I partied with Da Yoopers" and which feature a cartoon of a kneeling figure next to a toilet bowl, worshipping the "porcelain god," as Da Yoopers say. Linda Lou and I walk a few blocks to have a drink at the Royal Bar while we wait for her husband and children to join us at 11 PM for the shirt-tail parade where the volunteer firemen will compete in cross-dress and horse suits and strut in high heels and sequins down Main Street for the local crowds who will also duck, prance, and shout out when they get squirted with fire hoses by the firemen.

The genius of Da Yoopers is that of exploiting, making humorous, and writing their folk-country songs about the area. They make iconic characters out of local people and make most people laugh and feel nostalgic. Some locals feel ashamed that these local musicians from Ishpeming would make such fun of the working class mining culture that is a mix of Finnish-American and the other ethnicities—Cousin Jack, Italian, French-Canadian, Irish, Swedish, Norwegian. Da Yoopers have received complaints from some Upper Peninsula natives about their stereotypes, but that is what makes comedy. They are in the tradition of "Hello Mudder, Hello Fadder" Alan Sherman, Jackie Mason, and other ethnic humorists. They tell Finn jokes about Toivo and Eino, modifying Polish jokes for the purpose. They wear silly costumes, do amateur dances, and entertain their audiences. And their audiences love it.

One morning, visiting Da Yoopers Tourist Trap to buy the neighbor taking care of my cat back in Ohio a souvenir white pine nut bowl at a quite inflated price, I see one of Da Yoopers drive into the parking lot in a big white fancy car, in sunglasses, smoking a cigarette. She and my sister used to sing in the Ishpeming High School elite singing group, the mixed ensemble, and she's used her vocal talents well. I am glad for her. Heck, now, if good-ol'-boy and girl natives of the mining town of Ishpeming, fellow Ishpeming Hematites, can gross a million dollars in a mom and pop business that caters to baser instincts that make people laugh with embarrassment and the pleasure of recognition, more power to 'em, hey? eh? Right. You betcha!

Da Yoopers Deconstructed •

SHORT STORIES

"The Corner: Cleveland Location"
Photo: Steve Navarre

SNOWMAN

    Breaking trail into the woods, through snow calf to knee deep, on twelve year old cross-country skis, I puff as I ascend, the hill steep even in summer. I had to rent these boots because in my eagerness to get here, I forgot mine in Ohio, along with my gaiters and most of my wax. I only have warm snow wax in my ski bag, and this is cold snow, zero to ten degrees. I should be using white or blue wax, but I only brought green and red.
    Most skis are waxless these days, but I bought these because they were sturdy and wide, and I could break trail with them, as we used to do on those skis we used as children, with the leather binders and stub-nosed boots with ankle straps. These have a Finnish name—Laasanen—and are varnished, two-tone hickory and maple, beautiful to look at, not plastic. I've made crude gaiters from old, too-long, wool socks of my father, even though he quit skiing years ago. "Brittle bones," he says. "Creaks and cranks."
I cut out a heel and a toe hole and slipped them over the ski boots and up on my jeans. I need them today, with this deep snow.
    This neighborhood, like all neighborhoods in town, used to have a ski jump hill back here in the woods, and we boys used to build the bump from discarded Christmas trees. We all wanted to be like Joe Paul Perrault, who, when he came back from the Tenth Division ski troops in World War II, became the number one ski jumper in the country. I remember the scared thrill of soaring off the bump and onto the landing, trying to get my clumsy skis to land, hands like wings, one foot in front of the other, with only a few inches between the skis. The guys who got the most respect were the ski jumpers. I couldn't jump now if my life depended on it. Brittle bones. Creaks and cranks.
    As I tramp up the back yard hill, the backs of the skis stick

under the snow, and flop, wobble, so I have to raise my feet high and plant them firmly with each side step I take. We used to call this step "panking," and I guess they still use the word to describe the smoothing of landing slopes on jumping hills, as well as any sidestepping. I looked the word up in the dictionary, and it doesn't exist there, though I heard the word used the other day, by an old friend from the neighborhood, who was skiing with his wife on Christmas Eve afternoon. I met them as I took the ungroomed trail in the neighborhood woods.

Dave and Frieda were taking the trail in reverse. We stopped to talk. Dave and I exchanged memories of how these woods used to be only used by us, the neighborhood kids. I asked him whether he'd gone to the class reunion. "We all look old," he said. "It wasn't as much fun as the twenty-fifth and twentieth reunions." He said, "I panked some of the hills we came up, so you'll find them easier for you to go down. Lots of holes from people falling. Once one person falls, another one does, when the trails aren't groomed."

I began to get cold as fine sweat formed while I tramped the 6 kilometer, mostly uphill trail behind me. It soaked into my sweaty cotton underwear, so I said goodbye, nice to see you, and left. A person is never cold for long when he crosscountry skis, because when he gets cold he just starts moving again. I read about a couple in Colorado last year who had gone out on a 6 k. course and a blizzard hit. They kept skiing—it must have been awful, all that stabbing snow and the keening wind, and the disorientation one feels in winter woods where trails get covered up during blizzards—but they were found alive two days later, little the worse except for exhaustion, because they had kept moving the entire time. It is when one stops moving that one freezes.

That is why downhill skiing is so much colder than crosscountry, and the clothes are so much more insulated, padded. When I go downhill skiing out west every winter with the Toledo Ski Club, the wind perforates while I dangle with my skis hanging down, on the lifts going up and up the mountain. My fingers have old childhood frostbite in them, and this frostbite was exacerbated

• Snowman

fishing for salmon one fall on Lake Huron with my friend and so I cannot wear gloves downhill skiing, but have to wear huge padded mittens. I clutch my fingers into fists inside the palms of the mittens as I ride up chair lifts. When the tips of my fingers begin to freeze, the cold moves down the fingers and they turn white. I have to ski to the lodge and run my hands under lukewarm water until the color comes back into them. That is the price I pay for speed and fear and elation, pointing my metal downhill skis with my ankles encased in a plastic boot, molded into a forward position, my shoulders faced toward the bottom of the hill, down a mountain. Ski jumping, downhill, crosscountry. If I were younger I'd take up snowboarding and telemarking.

I like to crosscountry-ski alone these days, my middle-aged winter meditation time, though I do ski with a few friends, all of them natives of the Upper Peninsula, all of them at home on skis. As I crest the first high hill where the trail is so narrow I can neither pank nor herringbone, I take my skis off. At the top I put my skis back on and begin to tramp. My skis slip backwards on the narrow grade. Wrong wax. Blood begins to pound in my ears. The aerobic rush begins. Endorphins kicking in. I am at peace with the world thinking great thoughts.

Each year as I do this, I feel the inadequacy of whatever exercise I have been doing. This year I swam a half-mile several times a week, and walked quite often also. Not enough to keep my pulse from heating as I climb and climb. Lift, plant, glide. My poles guide me and I strike a rhythm. As I settle onto the snowed-over trail that is a wooded road during the summer, and get into the rhythm of the forward movement of skis and poles and body in snow, my mind and body begin the snow meditation. When I ski I feel as I do at the symphony. Mind wandering, yet held by the music. I pity music professionals whose critical training prevents them enjoying meditations during the concerts.

Today the sky is whitish grey, and a small, soft, not-grainy snow falls straight down, steady. There is no wind. This snow seems as if it won't build up much, but this has been the type of snow for the past few days, and the trail I made here yesterday is barely seeable. A few rounded pock-marks. A mini-drift over the edge of a pole mark. Eskimos have a hundred different names for snow. I notice the regularity of my pole plants, the memories of rhythms established when my growing muscles were making memories. I can skate, ride a bicycle, swim, climb rocks because of my childhood play in these woods.

It seems a shame to mark this chaste landscape with my body's weight on skis. The few animal tracks are of beasts that weigh a few ounces, and not a monster of over a hundred pounds, though my weight is distributed on the boards and I only sink six inches, and not to the ground. Someone has been snowshoeing on one of the trails crossing, and the shallow tracks look like wings of butterflies, overlapping. I don't like to snowshoe, though snowshoes are more efficient in deep snow. When I snowshoe, I feel like a baby with something in its pants. Someone has been snowmobiling, too. That is the only earthly good for snowmobiles—they leave good trails for crosscountry skiers.

Snow is my element. I remember when this realization came to me, about eight years ago, in Black Swamp. I and two friends were out after an Ohio blizzard, skiing on the golf course at the university. There is one hill in Black Swamp, called Phil's Hill, an artificial hill next to the freeway, made from displaced fill when the interstate was built, after the then-president of the university. As we climbed this short mound and faced west, ready to go down, to break trail, I felt unsullied elation even as my friends were expressing fear, as the phrase, "The wind in my teeth," came to mind. The speed, the freedom, the automatic way my knees bent, my hands just the right balancing geometry, on skis on snow, restored me. Snow still does that. Opens my wounds and then cauterizes my wounds. I feel a deep sob in my throat and I put my head back and it comes out, silently. Was that my wife leaving me again? My heart is rattling around in its cage. Grown men don't sob.

My father placed me in the snowbank outside when I was an infant, for my afternoon nap, to make me tough. There is a photograph somewhere in an album of my tiny, sleeping face,

• *Snowman*

swaddled in blankets and snowsuit and bonnet, in a wicker buggy placed in the snow. My parents had read somewhere in some Finnish homeopathic health book that placing a child for his nap in a winter snowbank made the child develop a resistance to disease. That book might be right. I never even had the flu. Though I do have the family disease.

In winter, the roads look like brown sugar. Depending on the amount of traffic on the street, the brown sugar snow is packed or loose. Snow banks get sheered by giant snow-go machines whose screws chew up and spew chunks into trucks that ride like baby whales next to their mothers, or like sidecars, and the geology of the winters can be traced in the cut banks, much like tracing the rings of a tree or the ages of a mountain range from a canyon. At corners, car hoods peep hesitantly out from behind the sheered banks and by March, if there has been no January thaw, antennas will have flags or flowers tied on them to warn people around the corner. In spring, though, during melting season, the past comes to haunt, as layer after layer peels off, and the litter of the winter is revealed. I don't like this filthy time at the end of winter and before the tulips. Cans, cardboard, plastic garbage, reminders of human carelessness and incompetence, revealed by the sun paring the snow, like old secrets surfacing when trusting lovers talk softly after lovemaking.

In winter, everywhere we go, during days when this small snow is falling, we have to brush the car off after going into a store. If we have ten stops to make, we have to brush the windows off ten times. Brushing the car becomes as automatic as igniting it. Watching people's styles of brushing snow, I notice three distinct types. Those who open the door, get the brush out, and circle the car, cleaning each window, are the detail people. Those who give a quick swipe to the front and side window with their mittens, cuffs, or bare hands, are the idea people. Those who get in and use their windshield wipers and hope the snow will blow off before they turn the first corner, are the risk-takers. My daughter is the third type, as was her grandmother, my mother. My daughter's mother was cowardly, a detail person making sure she could see in all directions. I vacillate between being the second and the third, depending on the depth of the snow.

Snow on roofs in the north is like charming clay tile in the south. Instead of red, white. The white slips over the edges of roofs, and gives even the most drab or shabby houses an elegance. The small bird feeder, hung by two strings, dangles in front of the window, with snow piled on its feeding perches. No birds find it. Our neighbor has three giant feeders, and all the birds who haven't migrated must visit his. The forlorn feeder filled with grains whips around and twirls in a sort of harmonic pendulum, its movement hypnotizing and entrancing. Perhaps the birds don't visit because they get dizzy. Perhaps such incantatory oscillation makes them drunk.

At St. Vincent De Paul's, the Goodwill Industries of the area, I shop for bargains. "Boots half-price. Still some wear in them." Crepe soles, rubber soles, hiking soles, corrugated soles, fur collars, fur-lined, Sorrels, swampers, shit-kickers. Thick laces, sturdy laces, leather laces, wide zippers, quilted ankles. Walking through town I count the different styles of boots I see, from floppy galoshes with clasps on them to high-heeled, elegant, knee-high gaucho boots with hard rubber soles. All good for walking in snow. The style on my students this year is defiant as ever. When I was a teenager, the style was white bucks with white socks pulled half way up the calves. The girls wore white polished tennis shoes with white socks. My sister's legs, when cold, still burst out in white dots of frostbite from that style. This year the teenagers are barefoot in loafers or ballerina shoes.

I watch two small children, one about seven, the other four, enter the yard in their snowsuits. Bundled so much their arms can't lie naturally, artificially fat, the children in snowsuits, stuffed like peppers, their little faces like flower buds peeping, roll as they bounce on a mound of branches left by a tree trimmer late last fall. The older pulls the younger one up and they waddle off, sliding on their boots down the bank, the smaller behind the bigger. The young one in a red snowsuit with yellow piping, has to pick his feet up high to plant them in the tracks of the older boy. Why is he

• Snowman

following the tracks at all? Why doesn't he just shuffle in the soft snow and make his own path? He wouldn't have to work so hard. The children run cumbersomely across the street to the newly plowed snow, and they amuse themselves by picking up fragile chunks hardened to the size of large boulders, as big as their chests, smashing them on the road. The snow chunks shatter. They jump on them, crushing them with their boots. I wonder when the neighborhood kids stopped making ski jumps.

On another day, coming back down into the back yard hill, I am struck that I, like the children, followed my own path, that this path I broke yesterday lies along the easiest fall line of the hill. The easiest way to go up. I made a path like a switchback road. It is a good path for ascending, but it is also a good path for descending. Any other way would make me slip, fall, crash, get snowy. I do not like to fall when I ski. That makes me angry. Part of it is pride, and when I fell once, skiing with my daughter, my daughter was gleeful. "Dad fell! Dad actually fell!" But my daughter didn't understand that part of it was also too many youthful falls that had injured my coccyx, twisted my knee so I wear a brace downhill skiing, wet my face, frozen my back where my waistband met my t-shirt, chapped my wrists, reddened my ankles climbing up the ski jump with my heavy skis over my shoulder, splayed on the icy steps, or grabbing the rope tow with my leather-palmed mitts.

Now I don't take any trail that will make me fall. Of course I am always surprised at how well I can make it down the high, hard hills on crosscountry trails, even with fear in my chest and fright in my eyes; by the time I get to the bottom I know I will stand it. Thinking back, I thrive on the rush of it. I am surprised at how well my childhood play has formed my skiing stance, how quickly I can regain balance when I hit a hole in the trail where someone else has fallen.

As I follow my own trail, I am aware that I have now marred the view, spoiling the immaculate back yard that can be viewed out the kitchen's back window while stirring food on the kitchen stove. Formerly untouched and pastoral, the yard covered with snow lights the house, even on dark days. The light is what is good about winter. Real winter, northern winter. It is lighter here than in Florida, where all the greenery absorbs light, doing photosynthesis. The worst month here in the north is bleak November, before the snow. In summer, without the snow, the yard is a tangle, with gout weed thriving, its murderous and tenacious roots undercutting and killing grass, the vegetables in the garden, the flowers in the planter. Wild maple suckers in the upper part of the back yard send shoots out all over, making a grove of saplings. My father spends much of the summer hacking the weeds away, but the scrap maple and the gout weed insist, preventing all but their own landscaping. Hardwoods can reproduce by shoots, where conifers can't. That is why the woods are overgrown with hardwoods, and there are fewer evergreens here than when I was younger. In summer the gout weed gets calf high, and garter snakes dwell beneath its cool canopy. With snow, the back yard seems at peace, the rampant wilding of the dominant vegetative marauders hidden, hibernating. I loosen the old swing, its chained seat caught beneath the depth, and thus I force it to mar the snow under the apple tree. As I ski down the last few yards, the metal clothesline, invisible in this flat light, almost garrotes me. "Science Teacher Slits Throat With Clothesline," the headline will read.

The despoiled landscape behind me, I push my pole into the hole that loosens my toe bindings, lift the skis up and clap them together, scraping the snow stuck on them with my mittens, leaning them against the wall of the patio, along with my poles. Inside, I peel my outer clothes down to my sweaty underwear, and then take off my longjohns, hanging them on the clothes rack, and, still cold and tingling, I stand, head back, under the soft warm spray of the shower in the basement in the sauna, feeling the cold release itself from my thighs and buttocks and face.

The mail has arrived. A note from Katherine on a funny, sexy card that compares a carrot to a penis. Katherine and I have been friends and sometime lovers for two years, but I wish she wouldn't send me notes at my father's. I don't want to be reminded of my normal world 600 miles away. My father asks, "What did Katherine have to say?" I answer, "She said her son wrecked her

Snowman

car and her ex-husband canceled the insurance." Katherine plays well on the courtly battlefield of all of us divorced who vowed to love and cherish.

A cup of warm cider and a cinnamon roll. A book, a chair, and it is only eleven A.M. A full day ahead. I feel good, pure, whole. Back when I was drinking, I'd wake up with the clouded head and fuzzed mouth of a smoker, sometimes even having to lean over the rim of the toilet to deposit the last of my stomach's heaving detritus. Hours later, I'd still be wandering in my sweats, still fuzzed, still clouded, lying around on the couch, calling in sick to my school, the lying drinker. I used the excuse of my wife running off with a fancy lawyer from the Gold Coast, but I was screwing around as much as she was. Back in the seventies, we called it "open marriage." What a joke. I would have used any excuse to drink, though. A classic case. Now my daughter doesn't have to worry about calling me after ten P.M.

Or even worse, I'd wake up in somebody's bed, some sad or wild woman I'd picked up at Max's Bar, where local professional singles hang out, and have to mutter my "I'll call you's" before getting home to throw up. One of them told me I made her feel ashamed, not calling. Well, I felt shame too, I wanted to tell her. And then I'd ignore them when I'd see one of them again--they numbered about thirty-five. I listed as many of them as I could remember one afternoon during my month in the hospital, trying to give them the dignity of having names—Sarah, Heather, Regina, Molly, Jackie—a regular potpourri of lovely women whose loveliness I couldn't see for my own exploitative pain.

All night the slow small flakes have been falling and yesterday's ski marks on the back yard are almost erased, leaving wrinkles with soft sides like rubber Halloween masks. This day the flakes fall bigger and slower but just as steady, and the white-gray sky brightens in the places where sun lurks. Streaks of blue appear. This gives a view of cloud movement, a slow swirl beyond the steady snow. Yesterday the clouds had been moving, I guess. Clouds are always moving. But the light had been such that they seemed still. The world seems timeless between ten and three when no winds blowing clouds are visible. Perhaps the world is timeless between those hours, the safe hours of midday.

Each day on my journey, my breathing gets better, and the pounding in my temples, as I reach the trail on top of the ridge above the lake, subsides faster. I still get my meditation high, though. I notice how the snow spreads itself on the branches, differently on different species of trees. On the crabapple, the deepest snow is on the thickest trunk and in the crevices near the trunk. On the tall white spruce—the Latin name comes to me from college dendrology class, *Picea glauca*—the snow is deepest and thickest near the centers of the branches, fanning out. On the trunks of the maples and oaks, the snow's compass shows me north and west. I will never lose my sense of direction in these woods.

Now, back, showered, cidered, I lie on my stomach on my old teenaged bed, gazing out the small windows just beneath the eaves through the icicles. They say if a house has icicles on it, it is not energy-efficient. None of us—my father, me, my sister—can afford to put a new roof on the house. Ridges on the icicles lie horizontal, and the pointed daggers vary in length, the longest about three feet long, the shortest a few inches. I bought a crystal glass candlestick that looks just like an icicle, made by a glass sculptor from Iitala as a wedding gift for my nephew one afternoon at the Finnish shop. All my crystal glass candlesticks are with my wife and her new husband.

The other day I pushed snow off the roof so the icicles wouldn't form. During warm spells when we were children, we were cautioned not to walk next to buildings with pitched roofs, because the snow would avalanche down and break the icicles off and the falling ice would hurt us, clunk us on the head and knock us out. This actually had happened to someone, people said. Of course, people also said that kids got polio from playing in leaf piles. The icicles drip, the water running through, to freeze at the bead of the last drop, the tip of the icicle.

I watch my father's neighbor, Frederick, whom I grew up with, still a bachelor working in the mine, living alone in the old, ramshackle house. He drinks, the rumor goes. Frederick was a

• *Snowman*

few years younger than I, so I'd only play with him when I couldn't find his brother, Clarence. The whole family has funny names like that. Clarence got in trouble with alcohol and lost his job at the mine. He's now downstate working maintenance at a shopping center, Frederick told my father. Today Frederick is holding on to his roaring snow blower, chook cap covered with flown snow. His long beard is caked, too. He wears a black leather jacket and baggy black work pants, like the guys at the gas station, with a chain and keys at his belt, and black leather gloves. I watch his fingers pull the lever forward and reverse, forward and reverse. The machine grinds the snow into fine, fine, misty white particles, flying in a plume cloud that sprays up and to the side.

The orange machine gives a sharp sound, not as loud as a snowmobile but louder than a truck without a muffler. Frederick trades plowing out the driveway for the baked goods my father gives him every time he bakes. Leaning against his caved-in porch is the omnipresent manual snow scoop, aluminum, with a u-shaped handle, used for pushing snow. On my father's roof is another snow-removing implement, with a handle about eight-feet long. For most of the winter, when I am not here, my father climbs a stepladder after the frequent snowstorms, to push the snow with this wobbly pusher, off the flat roof, pushing the snow over the edge, where it falls with an audible plop. I want to hire help for him and call an ad in the *Miner's Gazette*, the local newspaper, but he tells me not to rescue him; he can still do it, so why shouldn't he? We have a fight about it. My wife always let me rescue her; my father never does.

If the residents of the Upper Peninsula don't remove the snow from their roofs, leaks develop, and melted snow comes into the houses. A neighbor fell off a sloped roof last year and killed himself. He was seventy-five. My father is seventy-three, and still insists that this procedure is safe, because the roof is flat and he stays near the groove where it meets the slanted roof. The youth group at the church volunteered to do it for him, but he refused.

My father uses another snow shoveling procedure, as well, to shovel the heavy snowplow snow left at the end of the driveway, if Frederick doesn't get to it in time. My father takes a regular shovel, good for scooping poop in dog kennels, and with its edge, loosens the snowplow snow into his large aluminum push shovel, until the push shovel is almost filled. Then he pushes the shovel filled with snow, his hands on its U-shaped handles, across the street, lifting the handles to dump the snow on the opposite bank. No one lives across the street, so this works well.

Last Sunday morning in the church basement, during the coffee hour, where my father was showing me off to his friends—"See, my Jim from far away comes to visit me; I'm not alone all winter!"—I compared my father with my father's friends, who don't shovel snow off roofs, nor push snowplow snow. I noticed how young my father looked. Scarcely a wrinkle. Smooth skin. Today, we shovel together; I help my father move the snowplow snow in old Finnish boots brought over as a gift by some relative twenty years ago, with their pointed Lapland toes. He is wearing old gabardine pants, two wool sweaters with a turtleneck underneath, an old blue nylon padded jacket with elastic in back of the waist and a clasp belt, and a bumpy wool cap over his white-as-snow short hair.

"I can do it myself," is what my father says and we get into arguments. My father's mortality saddens me, so I avoid the confrontations. When he comes in, his cheeks are rosy and nose red. Naturally so. My father has never drunk nor smoked. The child of a raging alcoholic who used to come back in the middle of the night during a drunk, to steal and sell the chickens from the chicken coop for a bottle, he himself has never drunk much more than a sip of wine. So I had genes from both sides. That was a reason, but no excuse. Do I want to find my mother in the women I infrequently date and never go to bed with, now? Even Katherine. We haven't had sex for months. I am her escort at her office parties. What I liked about Katherine was she didn't call me up, but waited until I called her up. I'm still old fashioned that way. Am I becoming that archetypal bachelor, the old fart? My father is stubborn, crotchety, and independent as one. Will I have a belly, smelly breath, and my dead mother in my dreams?

• Snowman

Blue jays on the snow-covered picnic table in the back yard hop and peck. The three of them seem to be playing, bounding up to the maple tree, then to the table, and then to the black spruce. Perky heads turning in quick motions, their breasts are darker white than the snow, though in summer, their breasts look whiter. At my uncle Ingmar's farm where we went for sauna last week, the chickadees flew right onto our outstretched hands, perched on our mitts, eating feed. Those chickadees are my uncle's pets. He's never remarried after being widowed about the time of my divorce, though all the women at the senior citizen's center are after him. The world has many silent men watching birds. Frederick, me, my father, and Ingmar.

Today in the woods I stopped for a long time at the top, looking at the white lake far below over the cliffs, listening to my breath diminish, listening to my woods' winds. This lake had been drained to make a mine at the end of the nineteenth century, and then it had been allowed to fill up again, and the water level rose a few inches a year. Was it rising even now, beneath sinister ice?

Then I heard a thrashing, a beating of wings on the ground, behind a snowy stump, and thought I had flushed a partridge or a grouse. I heard a rasping sound as if someone were catching up to me on skis on the track I just made. The sound surrounded me so it was difficult to tell where it came from, yet it was as clear as at the theater at Epidaurus where once I heard a woman standing in the center of the stage floor whisper in German while I was seated in the top row. Then, above me, the logical conclusion. A downy woodpecker, *Picoides pubescens*, at the top of a spindly dead tree. I bent my head back to watch his rhythmic pecking, opening my mouth to speak to him, my lost and fouled-up young adulthood pecking with its hard bill eating insects out of holes in trees. Then I squinted and followed his silent, gulping flight out of sight, and heard in his absence the steady fall of globs of snow from the trees, and the small pummeling of small snowflakes on my jacket and the rattle of dead oak leaves. I returned home.

Ten years ago, before my major drinking began, my wife and daughter back at my parents' with the rest of the family, I and my oldest friend Billy Boy came here to ski on Christmas day. It had been a warm, sunny day. Dry brown maple and oak leaves rattled on branches; saplings creaked as if to make merry. Our skis clinked happily as we flung our bodies over crusted snow, whirred as we bent to hills. That day, the sky was colorado blue, and the light ended on gray rocks. Mountain ash berries on their branches looked like Christmas decorations through bare trees near the dark green cedar swamps. The squirrels that glanced across the track crossed trail with snowshoe rabbits, as we passed by the hats of acorns on the path.

That sunny day, we skied in sweater arms, bare-headed, and the snow sounded like wire tinsel, grainy, with slices of ice. We used red wax. We went fast, we crabwalked up the hills, the shadows of the twigs crisscrossing, a black and white oriental rug beneath us. The shadows of the sides of the ski trail grooves looked like mountain ridges from a distant plain. We felt no rejection there, in these woods of our place in the world. The ground received the snow in lumps, soft and sculpted mounds, a casual overlay. Logs looked like friendly puffy benches. Grass near rocks and trees insisted spring would come.

We passed some young boys who gleamed sweat on their lips and brows, but I and my old friend Bill had been very fit in those days. When we were kids back here, we used to pretend we were ski troops marching in line, the white-winged warriors of Finland during the Winter War with the Soviet Union. Or we used to imitate the Bietila brothers, men in our neighborhood, ski jumpers called The Flying Finns, who tramped every day in fast, efficient marching lines. That day we didn't pretend out loud, but as we trudged I know I thought it, and he probably did too. We leaned on our poles resting at the top of a particularly long hill climb, and we faced the sun on the slope, talking about our lives. Both of our marriages were in trouble. I told him I wanted to close up our modern open marriage. He said he wanted to have some experiences so he wouldn't be eighty-five rocking on the porch with only his wife in his memory.

Today, those times long gone, I miss my friend Billy, who

•*Snowman*

moved to California just before his divorce was final. Rash infidelity had done its job on both of us. He and I skied last winter, with Lenny, another of the neighborhood boys. Lenny can't ski this year; he got prostate cancer. Not one of us, nor our wives, has escaped disease, booze, drugs, cigarettes, job disappointments, sex with strangers, separations, messed-up kids living lives in childhood as confused as ours have been in adulthood. We used to think we were invulnerable, world class ski-jumpers from the frozen north. All of us, we were so hot after we walked on the moon and invented the birth control pill. Not one of my friends has escaped the consequences of the meltdown of the seventies.

Snow obscures pain with magnificent light and fragile sound. Snow numbs and freezes and paralyzes until it is thawed. Then it becomes water, the giver of life. At night, inside the house, it gets so bright when the moon is out, that I don't need a light to see the sweep and swell of earth near the window with the icicles creaking and the snow with its own crystal noise, falling down, falling down, obscuring and covering and renewing.

• • •

DOES IT SNOW IN VIETNAM?

Linda met Larry right before the first snowstorm, soon after the Cuban missile crisis in 1962, about a year before Kennedy was killed. The locals who commuted to the state college and the Air Force guys were downtown at the bars to celebrate the Air Force guys getting off alert. The local boys didn't like the Air Force guys, because they went after the local girls, but the local girls liked the Air Force guys fine. Seven guys for every girl was the ratio.

The Air Force guys were from all over the country, and it got so the local girls could tell a guy from California from a guy from Maryland just by the way he danced, before he even said a word and gave away his accent. California guys danced looser than Maryland guys. Many local girls ended up marrying Air Force G.I.'s, leaving the Upper Peninsula and settling down elsewhere. This is how it is wherever there are military bases.

Larry was from the Bronx, in New York City. He wore black pointed ankle-high boots or black pointed shoes and white socks, with cuffed pants, a thin black tie, and sunglasses, even after dark. Linda noticed him at once, the first night they met, when he came in. Who wouldn't? He seemed to be by himself, and smoked Pall Malls. He looked like a member of the rock and roll band playing there that night. The band, in suits and thin ties, swayed in sync with little steps thrown in, the guitars swinging. But this boy's hair was a little too short, so Linda knew he was Air Force.

After he asked her to Cha-cha, he asked her to have a drink. Linda didn't drink, but she had a coke with him, and a couple of puffs from his Pall Mall. They talked and talked. He was her first warrant officer, halfway between an officer and an enlisted man. And her first helicopter pilot, too. Well, not yet, but he planned to re-up and become one. His favorite book was Kerouac's *On The Road*. Linda's favorite book was Salinger's *Frannie and Zooie*. His favorite singer was Little Richard, and his favorite group was The Dave Brubeck Quartet. Linda's favorite singer was Edith Piaf, and she liked Dave Brubeck, too. He said he went into the Air Force because he got sick of college and thought he'd take a few years and see the world on Uncle Sam, then finish up on the G.I. Bill. He said he wanted to go to Columbia and study medicine later.

    He said he liked the college girls better than the other local girls. They knew more. Everyone here was so conservative, such hicks. Linda agreed. She wanted to go East someday, to New York City. Would he show her around? She let him walk her home even though he had a car. If she let him drive her home it would mean she was cheap, a pickup in a bar. He held her hand as they walked along the sidewalks past the sandstone police station, and he sang "Maria" to her. They each had seen the movie three times. He'd seen the play, too, on Broadway. She let him kiss her while they were sitting on a stone wall on the hill where her neighborhood was located. The first snowfall of the year was beginning. They caught snowflakes on their tongues.

    After they walked up the rest of the hill, she ran into the house, got the keys for her father's 1956 Ford station wagon, and drove him back down to the bar, where his battered Willys 4-wheel-drive Jeep sat alone in the parking lot, getting covered with snow. "You don't look like the Jeep type," Linda said.

    "I wasn't, but I am now," he said. "I love this country. I'm learning to fly fish." It was 5 A.M. and they had been talking all night. Linda's car pool would pick her up at 7:15 to go to the state college, so when she got home she didn't go to bed, but just sat and thought about him. She would spend many nights alone, thinking about him, but she didn't know that then.

    He didn't call her for three weeks and she almost died. By the time he did, there had been a huge snowstorm, just in time for Thanksgiving, and the deer hunters were very glad. Usually there is not very much snow for deer hunting season. Deer hunters prefer snow so they can track the deer easier. The Sunday night of

Thanksgiving weekend the snow came down. The radio was filled with news of students stranded on the way back to school downstate, caught on M-28 or U.S. 2, or out in the snow blowing across the fields or on the Seney stretch with lake effect snow off Lake Superior. But the college didn't cancel classes, so Linda picked her car pool up thirty minutes early. Five of them shared the driving, one day per week. Monday was Linda's day.

Sandy came out of her house late as usual, clutching her half-eaten toast spread with sticky jam, no boots on, slipping through the drifts. The others talked of dropping Sandy from the car pool because she had no consideration; they always had to wait for her and she was always getting people's cars sticky, but Linda was fond of her. They studied for literature tests together, to see who could get the higher "A." Linda headed them to Marquette and the soft snow flew up as the Ford station wagon solidly hit the drifts. The snowplows couldn't keep up with the snow. One of the keys to driving on snow is to keep a steady foot, to accelerate or decelerate slowly, so you don't lose traction. Linda's father had taught her that on the hills of town. "Shift!" he'd cry as she turned onto the bottom of a hill. "Downshift and keep it steady." Linda rarely got stuck.

Larry called her that same night, said he'd been working swings, but had been thinking of her and did she want to go out on Friday? Did she.

She taught him to crosscountry ski that year of their courtship. They packed cocoa and peanut butter and banana sandwiches into her father's old World War II-vintage knapsacks, with the leather straps cutting into their shoulders, and they skied up behind her house through the sparkling woods in the sun, over snowfields, under clean skies. She told him what wax to use, and how to tramp so he wouldn't slip back down the trails he'd made. She told him to be the boss of his skis. That was the secret of skiing. Don't let the skinny little devils get away from you. Control them. Just like driving in the snow. Plant your legs solidly. Use your poles like levers, in front. Place them, to pull with maximum efficiency when you pank up the hill. A little practice and they won't cross on you. They'll obey you.

Even though he was a natural athlete, from all the gang fights, he'd joke, he took awhile getting the hang of it, having two long planks attached to his feet, and he'd forget to dig in his edges or to bend his knees in gulches. He had trouble stopping and would have to sit down to avoid trees. He looked very comical, and she often turned her head to suppress giggles at the sight of him. "Wait until I get you to the city, lady! They we'll see who thinks what is funny. I'm going to abandon you in the subway and see if you can find your way home." His jeans would be soaked from falling down so much, and Linda's would still be pristinely dry, as she waited for him to catch up. Even with wet jeans he took her breath away, with his cocksureness.

•

Years later, when they could afford downhill skiing in the Rockies, he'd zip past her as she slowly snowplowed down the wide slopes, shushing by her, leaping into spraying stops in front of her. This was after she'd learned her fear of snow.

•

By 1969's winter, Chicago had happened and everyone had been assassinated. Linda and other professors at the state college called themselves doves as they had meetings and marched and signed petitions. As the wife of a helicopter pilot, Linda got first preference for teaching courses at the Base, and she drove there, passing the B-52's lined up, painted flat sky blue on their bellies and camouflaged with splotches of green and shades of brown on top. It always bemused her to know that these were the very bombers that all the fuss was about, the silent killers dropping fire from the skies; that here in peaceful, wintry Upper Michigan they rested in innocent rows at the Strategic Air Command base; that next week or tomorrow they could be above North Vietnam dropping firestorms and death, and probably would be.

Another cold February day. Outside, Linda turned the locking hubs, putting the vehicle into four-wheel drive. She climbed up into the old Jeep, her high-heeled teaching boots turning at the ankle. She clapped her gloved hands, wiggling her fingers, woofing her breath into clouds that soon frosted the windows. She pressed the starter with her thumb, her fingers now curled into her palm, the fingers of the gloves flopping, wet and freezing. She pumped the accelerator. The defroster blew a feeble shoot of air, dripping a vertical puddle on the windows. She waited for the engine to get just a little warm, and for the heater to heat.

Her small son waited patiently in the seat next to her, his legs stuck out in the stiff red snowsuit, his arms and mittened hands at his side, touching the seat. He couldn't turn his head to her because his hood couldn't turn, and so he resorted to speaking from the sides of his eyes and mouth, looking like a miniature gangster. "Mama, are we going to make it out of the driveway?"

"I've got it in 4-wheel." She noticed her legs getting red in their nylons. Her short skirt was not much protection. But fashionable she would be.

She wrestled the 4-wheel shift lever and eased the clutch, and the Jeep tires grabbed the crunchy snow as sure as spring was coming, and they moved down the long unplowed road from the trailer court where they lived, to the highway. At the highway she stopped and scrambled back down to turn the locking hub back to regular drive. Then they drove along, up high, higher than the slipping cars on the glassy highway, almost as if they were in a low-flying helicopter.

"Does it snow in Vietnam, Mama?"

"No, it's very hot. Jungle. Lots of trees, like here, though." Her breath puffed out as she answered him.

"Will my daddy have a letter for us when we get home?"

"Perhaps. If the mail can land at the airport after last

• *Does It Snow in Vietnam?*

night's snow."

They drove along past the frozen waves of Lake Superior, into town. This drive into the city was always beautiful, whatever the season. She was glad Larry talked of settling here after he got out of the Air Force. She couldn't picture herself in the Bronx, though she liked visiting there, taking the subway into Manhattan, strolling along Fifth Avenue past the Metropolitan Museum, on a sunny day. "Looks like I'll make my ten o'clock after all."

"That's good, Mama. Will we get to play outside in the snow today?"

"Son, if Mrs. Maki can get all you kids into your snowsuits and if you can find your own boots, you'll go outside, I'll bet." Mrs. Maki and her helpers stuck twenty children's fat legs into snowsuit bottoms and forty stiff arms into snowsuit tops and all those recalcitrant thumbs into mittens pinned to sleeves. They slid all those rubber-soled shoes into plastic bags and then into boots that always had stuck zippers, all so that twice a day the children could stand around like stiff robots in the yard, trying to run and play, but hampered so much by their snowsuits that they could do little that was graceful and normal for toddling children. Then, twice a day they had to undress them all.

They pulled up to the nursery school, and Craig tumbled out of the Jeep and waddled up to the door. He had begun to insist on going in by himself, because he thought he was getting older now. Besides, he got a kick out of ringing the doorbell. She watched him as he ran clumsily up the walk, doing his helicopter imitation sound and trying to whirl his snowsuited arms.

"When will my daddy be home, Mama?" he asked every night as she kissed him before sleep.

"On leave? In a few months. But he'll be going back. He's got eighteen months left, Craig," she would say.

She passed the bombers once a week on her way to her humanities class. A navigator in her class wrote a theme about a napalm drop from one of those B-52's. "We are so high up," he wrote, "and the plane is dark. Nothing but the smoothness of the flight and the lights on the instruments. I am isolated from the rest of the crew. Chit-chat on the earphones. I find the right coordinates and tell the pilots. Someone presses something. There isn't any sign that we have dropped. Far below, a pinpoint of fire color, but real small. Most of the time we are above the clouds and we can't see anything. We turn around and go home. We have a drink at the officer's club before we go to sleep. Being a navigator in the U.S. Air Force has nothing to do with what you bleeding heart liberals think it is. I'm in the war, supposedly fighting, but I'm as removed from it as the rest of you people up here in the U.P., doing your pinko picketing at the Post Office."

She read the essay to the other men in the class. They were mostly enlisted men who had joined the Air Force, hoping to be stationed stateside, and they were. They held technical jobs like airplane mechanic E-4, and radar technician E-3, trying to get a few hours of college credit in. The navigator had a college degree but it was in engineering and he wanted to become a Renaissance man, he said.

"What do you think of this essay?" The men complacently said it sounded like a good tour to them, better than being a grunt in the Army.

"Don't you see the moral distance here?" She pleaded with these bland young men. "Someone presses something. And what are the consequences of pushing that starter button? Don't you care that people are getting killed for nothing? Don't you care that we're in a war that isn't even declared?"

"Lady, I'm trying to save my own ass. Just didn't have a deferment like you liberal college types, that's all."

"What does your husband think, him out there flyin' helicopters and you here safe and warm, talkin' to us like this?"

She read them from Larry's letters, passages about picking up maimed and burned soldiers, children in rags, adults in tears; she read passages describing his fear of dying for no reason, and his fear he would never see her and Craig again, never take the A train again, never fly fish on the Dead River again.

"Listen, this is written by a middle-class American G.I.," she would say. "I believe in George Washington and the flag and all that, too," she would say.

Some of them would get explosively angry, standing up and shouting at her. But this was certainly humanities in humanities class, she explained to her department chair who'd gotten a call from the Base coordinator. Other students would sit sullenly. She got a few anonymous calls calling her a traitor to her man and her country.

She was not asked back to teach an extension course at the base the next semester. She wrote letters to Larry telling him what she was doing and he wrote back and said he wished he could be there, joining her. She read anti-war poetry at a rally at the college and encouraged students to burn their draft cards. She wrote letters to her legislators and signed them as the wife of a serviceman. Such senseless and random death and destruction as from the lofty and lethal B-52's cannot be tolerated. Please stop in the name of human rights, she wrote.

•

"Sure is a lot of snow up here," he said, brushing it from his shiny black flapping overshoes with the broom. "I'm from Tennessee myself, we don't get mucha this white stuff at home," brushing the snow from the shoulders of his heavy fur-lined Air Force parka.

"Would you like some coffee?" Linda said, as he bent to pull his boots off.

"No'm. I won't be here long. My wife makes me take my boots off the minute I come in the house, just habit, I guess."

He looked out the front window of the trailer, acting awkward at being here, a big, red-faced boy playing soldier. "Those kids shore have a good hill built out there," pointing to the seven foot snowbank where the trailer court kids were pushing each other off in King of the Castle.

"Yes. Kids and snow, you know. They love it. They never seem to get cold, and it seems to make them healthy, at least it did me. I love the snow, too. I grew up around here."

"Yeah, I heard you're a local. Came back home to be near your folks. Which one of them is yours?"

"The one in the red snowsuit," Linda said, coming and leaning next to him on the counter, pointing out the front window.

"Cute little tyke," he said.

"That's not what you're here for, is it?" Linda said. "To admire my son and to talk about why I moved here? What did the Air Force want to see me about?"

"Well, 'm." He cleared his throat. "It's your picture in the papers again. Makin' that speech at that there anti-war teach-in at the college," he said. "And then we got another photograph of you carryin' a sign at the Post Office, that said—. He peered at the photograph. "War is not Healthy for—"

"War is not Healthy For Children and Other Living Things," Linda finished, interrupting him in her best supercilious professor's voice, though she was trembling inside. "It's the slogan of a group called Another Mother for Peace. I'm in the local chapter, and we marched last Mother's Day, with our children."

"Someone sent us a copy of that one. And we ignored it, but this year you've been in the paper three times."

"So what?"

"Well, your husband. Being a G.I. and all. It doesn't look good for a military wife to act up like that. We got to keep a united front, stand behind our men."

"You sound like a black and white World War II movie."

He flushed and his mouth turned tough.

"I'm sorry," Linda said in a kinder tone. "That was uncalled for. Lieutenant, I am standing behind my man. I"m trying to help stop this war, and get him home. Do you know what he's probably doing right now? Going in under fire and pulling out wounded soldiers."

He continued as if he hadn't heard her. "So the colonel told me to come and mention it to you, nice-like."

"Well, Lieutenant—" She peered at his nameband.

• Does It Snow in Vietnam?

"Greenwale. You've mentioned it. We thank you for your concern."

"Are you going to be more careful?"

"It shouldn't matter to the Air Force what I do. I don't live on Base. I'm an American citizen with freedom of expression. Haven't you heard of the First Amendment? I'm not hurting anyone by speaking and marching."

"It don't look good," he insisted. "Freedom of speech. Why we're fighting communism.

"I'm just exercising my rights."

"You aren't doing your husband any good. Why, what must he think of you?"

Linda had enough sense not to mention that Larry was every bit aware of what she thought, and she had the urge to show his letters to this man, as she had read them to her classes. Being a disloyal wife? She wanted to prove to him exactly how loyal she was. "I'm against the war for personal as well as political reasons, Lieutenant," she said. "It took my husband away from his family. All he wanted to do was fly helicopters. Not fly them in Vietnam. He hardly knows Craig at all, and he's almost three. He could get killed, or captured, anytime. And for what? A civil war that's been going on for hundreds of years. Not even our fight. A damned civil war!" She heard her voice getting louder, as if she were making a speech.

"Yeah. Well. You're dead wrong. And you don't need to give me another one of your speeches. I read them, they sounded just like the ones they were giving at my college."

"But you were one of those in ROTC, weren't you, Lieutenant? You would never go to a peace rally, would you?"

"Our instructor assigned us to go or I never would have," he said. "You don't have to believe what people are saying about us. We're people too. Those bleeding heart professors and long-hairs don't know which end is up, to go and hear them speak," he said. Linda could feel ire. This kid was calling her narrow-minded, when it was he, and his kind, who were.

"I heard you speak before," he continued. "You're pretty

good, you really get people's emotions het up," he said. "We got a tape of you at that rally."

"A tape?"

"Your file. Why I came to talk with you. You're being watched by Washington."

"Washington?" Linda was shocked. Here? In the U.P.? Then the anger came. "Washington? What do I care about Washington! Let them arrest me! *Put* me in jail. Put me on tape. Put me on file! Try me. I've done nothing illegal. What country is this, *any*way?"

"You liberals think you know it all, that you've got right. Well, if you've got right, we've got might," he said. His smug face.

"Let them stop this war. This is an immoral, imperialistic, fucking war, and I don't care who's got me on file for saying it! You can go and tell your colonel that! Tell that to Hoover! Tell him to take all the tapes and pictures he wants. Took pictures of me? Who do you think you are? Who do you fucking think you are?"

"Ma'am, I never heard a nice lady say that word."

"What word?" Linda stopped. She remembered. She shouted, "Fucking? Well, I'll say it again. This is an immoral, imperialistic, fucking war, Lieutenant." She walked over to him, picked up his boots, and pushed them to his chest, beckoning toward the door. "Now get out of here."

He resisted and stood up to her and seemed about to raise a fist to hit her. "Lady, *you* are what is wrong with this country! You and all those other commies, hippies, and nuts! You and your kind is why we have to fight in 'Nam!" He pushed her. She had stepped into his space and he was flailing at her to get away. "What kind of wife are you? Your own husband fighting and you act like the bra burners and the filthy-mouthed libbers!" He was yelling very loud. He snatched his boots, not bothering to bend to put them on. He stepped out onto the ice-covered steps and slammed the door. He slipped down the path on his slick soles, his voice raging, as he shouted back at her.

"If my wife ever acted like you, you smartassed, you— college professor, you dope freak, I'll bet—I'd-I'd beat the shit out

• *Does It Snow in Vietnam?*

of her!"

He slammed the door of the blue Air Force official car, started the motor, jammed the gears into reverse, tromping on the accelerator, spinning the wheels backward too fast, too fast, as if he were peeling on pavement and not on snow, a southerner who didn't know the finer points, not seeing the small red nylon sled of a boy belly bumping behind the car after being pushed off the top of the King's Castle.

．　．　．

DEER CROSSING

"Upper Peninsula," the sign across the highway said, and the next minute the speeding car with its automatic pilot set on 66 mph, hurtled onto the Mackinac Bridge. She tapped the brake and slowed to the requisite forty-five miles per hour, relieved, now. Home. The lights hung on the graceful suspension arches reminded her of that other bridge, the Verrazano, which she had crossed this morning at 6 A.M. Two noble bridges, the Mackinac, built in 1957, its main span 3,800 feet, and the Verrazano-Narrows, built in 1964, its main span 4,260 feet. She had driven 900 miles since crossing the Verrazano, and now had only 200 to go. Home.

She paid the $1.50 toll and drove up the curved ramp, turning towards U.S. 2. 9 P.M. She'd be pulling into the driveway about 12:30. She stopped to fill her travel mug with a caffeine hit, to use the bathroom, and to fill the gas tank. The trip had cost thirty dollars so far. She'd taken $200.00 out of her Citibank branch this morning before heading out. She had to slow down to fifty-five now that the freeway had run out. She passed a pickup truck going forty-five, and turned on her brights. Not much traffic. Saturday night. The drunks wouldn't be out until the bars closed.

Ground fog began appearing as she turned up highway M-117 through Engadine, and onto the Seney stretch. She had to use the dims because with the brights, the fog swirled and she was blind, although the moon shone clearly high above, and she could even see stars, something she missed in New York City. The deer crossing signs were more frequent now, black silhouettes of prancing bucks on yellow heraldic diamond shaped shields. The narrow bridge where she'd almost been squeezed into the abutment by a snow plow last winter on her way back to New York popped up out of the fog. She was afraid that a deer would come onto the road in the instant of darkness between her and an approaching car, just as their dims began to meet.

She had hit three deer in her life: one twitched in its death throes, and she had had to batter it on the head with a shovel in order for it to die. It had been a pregnant doe that had leaped over a snowbank over by Iron Mountain. When the state police came, they gave her the deer, loaded it into her trunk, and her husband had dissected it, butchered it on the lab table at the Department of Natural Resources, and they had eaten venison for months. The second deer had run into the woods to lie wounded in the darkness, after smashing her fender and breaking her window. The third had glanced off her rear and walked off unharmed.

Watch for their eyes, she'd been warned. Deer always look at the lights. One can see the neon yellow-orange of their eyes before they cross. Her hand gripped the wheel and she scanned the sides of the road in the dims-lit ground fog. There! she saw them, ready to run across in front of her. She felt the energy of fear. Fear of deer.

Back in New York City she had to watch out for muggers, had to cross the street if someone started following her from the subway station, had to watch for their eyes looking at her too long. Fear of strangers, young males, young black males especially. Fear of ragged winos rapping on her windows on Houston Street. Fear of strong, evil-smelling mad rapists breaking into her apartment and waking her in the dead of night. Fear of what would happen to her now. Fear of other people led all of New York City to live behind locks and bars.

Home. Go home. Leave now. Take your sick leave and just say no. No, you can't watch me publicly impaled on your spear, Dr. Betts. I'm not coming back to finish my contract. Two thousand people—parents and their children—watching to see whether she'd break. One hundred and fifty teachers watching her. When they fire you in the schools, they watch you twist and burn publicly. Now she and the other principal had made the front page of the New York *Times*, Local Section. Her friend Meg had been fired from an ad agency recently. The word came at noon, and Meg cleaned her desk and was gone by two, never to see the deliverer of the news again, no prolonged public humiliation.

Every day the calls, the letters, the confused parents, the forlorn children. "Why?" The union head, the union, the teachers, why? She and the other principal, her counterpart, both not renewed. Why? Rumors and plots. Newspaper reporters' bylines, with allegations and investigations. Why would Dr. Betts do that? All the usual urban explanations were offered. Racism. Jealousy. Insecurity. Psychopathology. Cronyism. Corruption.

The fog floated behind her and she sped, alone, past the turn by Lake Superior. Now, as always, she felt truly North. People "down below" the Mackinac Bridge said they were going "up north" when they were merely going to Traverse City or Gaylord. That was south to true northern Michigan people. Out of the fog behind her she saw flashing lights. A speeding ticket? Swooping to fill her rearview mirror, it became an ambulance. She pulled off to let it pass. Someone was being rushed to the hospital at the medical center sixty miles away. The remoteness of the area hit her as she imagined the medical emergency crew working on that poor soul over that long hour to expert help.

She tried to follow the ambulance, thinking that it would scare all the deer crossing away, but it was going seventy-five. Too fast. Eerily sweeping, blinking a dim red-orange in the fog, its lights disappeared and she completed the trip alone, taking familiar back roads, through tunnels of woods grown up to the berm.

Her mother had left the porch light on. Her trip indicator rolled up to 100. She'd driven 1100 miles since morning. She stumbled out of the car and received her mother's concerned hug. "I need a glass of wine," she said.

She slept until 10 A.M. and they went to the old Finnish Lutheran church where she had been confirmed. She hadn't gone to church seriously for fifteen years. Sitting next to her mother she took in the medieval ritual performed by an earnest young minister who didn't have a Finnish name, and every time they sang a response, tears choked her throat and she couldn't sing. By the time they got to the offertory, "Create in me a clean heart, O God/ and renew a right spirit within me," she had to take off her glasses and wipe her wet cheeks.

"That's just the Holy Spirit working," her mother said confidently with the calmness and candor of someone who is at peace in her world. Their mother performed her daily devotions at daybreak each morning, sitting in the front window. Often their children, early risers, would join Grandma there, calmly chatting, sketching the Pines across the street, in easy companionship with such dawn spirituality.

From New York City, she often pictured her mother there, enfolding her faraway children and grandchildren in the peace and grace that radiated abroad from study as her mother painstakedly worked from both the Finnish and the English Bibles, comparing the languages, translating, studying. She was the only Finn, in fact, the only Scandinavian where she worked, though one of the first graders was half Swedish and half Jewish. If she hadn't been white, she'd have been called a minority.

They walked in the woods. It was the first time she had been here in May for many years, and the winter-trampled brown leaves were beds for thousands of mayflowers and dog-toothed violets, their delicate whites and muted yellows volunteering first to greet the late northern spring. The trilliums weren't quite out. The mottled purple and green leaves of the dog-toothed violets sprouted everywhere, fields and fields of them. They looked for morels everywhere under oaks and apple trees that had gone wild, but had no luck. It had been a dry spring.

Her friend Karen's husband had gone out into the woods and committed suicide near here, shot himself in the head with a shotgun, a few years ago. Karen had threatened to leave him, and take the children. He was a true Finn. He came to the woods to die, they said. Once she had seen a Finnish movie with subtitles, and it had been about a city dweller finding a rabbit in the woods, taking it to the city, and then moving with the rabbit back to the woods.

Near the cross country ski trail, they found fiddleheads, light-green, coiled. They snapped off the tops of three of them, and shared the tender hairy bitterness as a woods-walk snack. In the swamp they found marsh marigolds, the assertive greens and blatant yellows reflecting themselves in the mirror of the dark brown tannic water. As kids they called the swamp flowers cowslips and were surprised to learn their names in a wildflower guide. She ritualistically and foolishly picked some cowslips, knowing the stems would wilt by the time they got home.

All the while she talked with her mother, wondering whether she should just take her sick leave, since she had seventy unused days of it, look for a new job from here, have them send her paychecks here, pay her rent from here, pay off her bills from here, home. She could go back in August to clean out her apartment. Her mother said, "You're swimming through deep waters, aren't you?"

Her mother said she should think twice about such a move. That might be cowardly and she might not like herself for doing it. Her mother said all those New York people were looking at her for strength in their confusion and mourning back there in Manhattan. "End it with dignity," her mother said.

She talked about her fear. She said she didn't have any more strength. "You'll find it," her mother said.

They walked onto the top of the bluff near the power lines and saw the chain of seven small, pure lakes that stepped down, flowing one into the other, for several miles. In the spring in the woods one can see everything for a few weeks, until the leaves come out. The leaves come out just about the time the lilacs are ready to bloom. That wouldn't be for several weeks. When she got married, she had lilacs whose smell filled the old church. A June bride. Years ago, when she had been an innocent. That night they watched "60 Minutes" and Jessica Fletcher, and read companionably on the sofa.

The next day, she got up early and quietly drank morning coffee next to her mother. She read Mary Oliver's poems while her mother read the Bible. Then she called in sick long distance, and her sister came over and they all went out to camp, lit the sauna, and dared each other to run naked into the cold lake that had just last month had ice on it. Their mother didn't run, though. Her sister

Deer Crossing

agreed with her, and they argued with their mother that she should stay here, at home, and not go back to New York City. "Why give such a courtesy to that Dr. Betts woman who got rid of them?" her sister said. "Laurel, you don't owe that school anything. Show them. Just use up your sick leave. Plead mental harassment."

"Show them what?" her mother said. "That she can't take it?" Her mother said that wouldn't be right, she wasn't really sick, just shamed. "You've got nothing to be ashamed of, while that woman will live with your blood in her throat for the rest of her life. Show those New Yorkers some Finnish *Sisu*," her mother said.

They sat, the three of them, in the sauna, sweating, putting their faces in washcloths, pouring water over their heads, then washing each other's backs, throwing water on the rocks and running into the lake. The intensity of talk got to them, so they stopped and basked, silently, in the radiant heat, their feet up, their backs against the wood, the window open a little for oxygen. Their father had built this sauna stove before he died, and their husbands had built the sauna and the camp, a little each summer, when they came on vacation.

They rested afterwards, and their mother heated her famous pea soup on the old wood stove. They had it with thick slices of her Finnish rye bread, made with mashed potatoes, among other ingredients. They played gin rummy for three. Their mother beat them. She was a real rummy shark. They drank strawberry pop, as their grandmother had. For dessert there was a thin blueberry sauce and jelly roll. Their faces were shiny, their hair plastered to their heads, their cleanliness scrubbed into their skins. Back home, after her sister had gone back to her husband and kids in the neighboring town where she was a professor at the local state college, she and her mother began to talk about the problem again.

"Mother, I've lost my husband, I've lost my child, and now I've lost my job. What more can I lose?" she argued, with what was beginning to seem like strong self-pity.

"You have your health and your brains and your talent," her mother said." And you didn't lose your child. He's just living with his dad. And all those people will hold you in their memories. Their memories own you. Let dignity rule. Go to the end." The infuriating strength of this implacable and gentle woman made her angry.

She slammed the door when she went out to take another walk, this time up the bluff across the street. The familiar path took her feet over the slippery hematite iron and jaspillite rocks, onto the pine needles, onto the grassy flats, and then on up, onto the dome of the bluff where she sat on the rock outcroppings where she had played for hours, imagining herself in the jungle or on the range. She sat, her knees almost up to her face, facing west, and watched the sun set in fire and afterglow. She could see so much better in spring. She sat there for a long time, enveloped by rosy lavenders and peaches and pinks, staring west, among friends.

The darkness took the technicolor away. It had been dark in New York an hour ago, and in an hour it would be dark in Rapid City, and in another hour it would be dark in Denver. She could send her fear and hatred, her bitterness and sense of betrayal, to Los Angeles and out into the Pacific Ocean sooner than she could drive back to New York City, even to the Mackinac Bridge across the nighttime country looking for the neon eyes of deer on the side of the road. It occurred to her her fear could go west, with the sun. It would crash there with the sun on the International Dateline.

Smiling at the thought of the impact of what a red and orange and yellow crash that would be, she went down the bluff knowing the way instinctually, as easily as she knew how to ski, to skate, to find a fiddlehead or to build a fire in the right sheltered spot in the woods. Her mother and she had tea and watched the old movies channel.

Now, whether or not she got a new job there, she also knew how to walk aggressively on an urban street, how to take the subway, how to park in a spot that looked too small, where, when, and what to eat, how to carry her purse so she wouldn't be pickpocketed, Off-Broadway and off-off, Lincoln Center and Symphony Space, the Film Forum, BAM, which room was the best in the Metropolitan Museum of Art, galleries in Soho. If she could make it there, she'd make it anywhere.

She left early the next morning and took two days this time, stopping at her son's father's house in Lower Michigan to tell them. By the time she crossed Pennsylvania the deer crossings weren't dark yet, the New Jersey Turnpike was all lit up, and the tolls on the Verrazano were still four dollars, dues paid when leaving town.

• • •

GRASS FIRES

Suppertime, and Mr. Peterson limps down the slanted sidewalk next to the old house. He leans against the thick maple, his feet covered by first windfallen yellow leaves, and he yells, in the loudest voice anyone has ever heard, for his children to come home. That is his work nowadays: he keeps track of his children.

"Dalton Murray! Wright Laughlin! Cranston Philip! Clayton Clifton! Beckwith Blake! Wendy Mamie!" The neighborhood, still in the twilight, echoes.

"Get your asses in to supper," he growls to the two little girls playing house under the high porch, among the stacked logs for the wood stove in the kitchen. Abigail Nellie and Wendy Mamie scutter quickly up the cracked walk, into the back porch, slamming the loose screen door, to the odorous kitchen, smelling of yeast and sweat.

The neighborhood children are scared of Mr. Peterson because of how he yells and swears, and because of his limp. His own children are scared of him, too.

Mr. Peterson pulls out a jackknife and slices a twig from the bayberry bush next to the maple. As the children run home from the hills and woods of the neighborhood, he cuts menacing swaths at them with the knife, and he switches them with the twig.

Clayton Clifton is the last one home, as usual. "Get your ass in here, Clayton Clifton!" The small boy trips as he runs up the sidewalk. His overalls are muddy, and they have holes in the knees. The back pockets are frayed, and they flap.

The house is ramshackle, with siding falling off, and no one sits on the high front porch because it creaks as if it will collapse. The boards are rotting and no one wants to fix them.

Mr. Peterson limps up the sidewalk laboring and puffing,

pulling himself straight-legged, one step at a time, up the steep cement steps, both hands on the pipe railing. Mrs. Peterson, in a flowered dress held with loose buttons, and a floured apron, her belly and breasts bursting and round, waits for him, smiling and friendly, and she moves to help him up the last step. As he hoists himself up, he swats her away, then pushes her stomach so that she cringes, but she still smiles.

Their children have the fanciest names in a neighborhood filled with Shirleys and Bettes and Errols and Roys. Their grandma, Mrs.-Mrs. Peterson, as everyone calls her, gave them the names. She heard them in England, where she worked after she left Sweden and before she came here to be a maid for the mine bosses, back before World War I, and her name, they say, is Sonja. Mrs. Peterson's name is Princess, and not a nickname either, Mrs. Peterson tells the neighborhood children. Mr. Peterson's name is Siegfried Thor, but everyone who is a grown-up calls him Blackie because he is one of those Swedes with black hair and brown eyes, the Laplander showing through, they say.

Mr. Peterson used to work underground at the Mather C iron mine, until he got laid up. The shaft car fell down the shaft on the night shift when he was in it. Mr. Peterson stays home now and he drinks beer with the neighbor men who work in the mines, in the back yards on Saturday nights, in the summer after supper and after the Finns have taken their saunas.

Clayton Clifton sits in the grass listening to the men talk and he gets sips of beer from them. So do the other boys. The men talk about old times and about The Company and about the price of steel.

Clayton Clifton mostly plays with Maxine, the kid next door, and with Beckwith Blake, his little brother. Everyone thinks Beckwith Blake is weird because he has buggy eyes and he drools and he is in the slow room at the Cleveland School. Clayton Clifton is supposed to take Beckwith Blake everywhere with him, to look after him, but Maxine takes care of him sometimes while Clayton Clifton goes up the top of Ore Street to play baseball on The Flats, the only flat field in the neighborhood, well not flat really, it has a rock outcropping by second base. Maxine is willing to take care of Beckwith Blake because she told Clayton Clifton she thinks Clayton Clifton is cute, the only kid in the neighborhood, with all the blondes, with black hair and brown eyes.

Clayton Clifton hasn't come home yet. Mr. Peterson keeps yelling, and it is way after dark, but Clayton Clifton hasn't come home because he is home already, up in his and his older brother Dalton Murray's bedroom smiling and giggling. He is thirteen and he has had three cans of beer from the six-pack he found under the jumble of blankets and underwear under Dalton Murray's bed.

Dalton Murray is twenty, and he is making out with Carol, their brother Wright Laughlin's new sister-in-law. Carol is eighteen and comes over in the afternoons, now that she's a part of the family, and she and Dalton Murray have a few beers while Dalton Murray tries to go all the way with her.

Carol has a soft, fat belly, and she has pimples, but she laughs a lot, and so everyone has to laugh too. She used to be a waitress, but now she is getting help from the Welfare for her baby. The baby's father said he was going down to Waukegan to try to get a job for American Motors, and he never came back, so Carol is stuck. When she has a few beers, while they are kissing, she always asks Dalton Murray if he will marry her. Dalton Murray says he will if she lets him go all the way. Clayton Clifton hid under the bed in the junk once and heard them screw.

Clayton Clifton quits school on April 29, the day after his sixteenth birthday. He has never learned to read good, and the teachers are mean. He is in the eighth grade with all the little kids, and they tease him and call him Clay Cliffs. He stayed back a few years and all the kids he started school with are juniors, so he'll never catch up. Clayton Clifton figures he can get a job in the mines and get enough money to marry Carol. Carol still comes over every afternoon, even after Dalton Murray married that girl from Negaunee. She drinks a few beers with Clayton Clifton and they screw. Clayton Clifton has been skipping school for a month.

He and the Whiting boys, who live up by the Stone Wall, next to The Pit where the mine used to be, go up into The Woods, behind

Grass Fires

the houses in the evenings, to shoot birds with their .22s. Last night they had a fifth to celebrate Clayton Clifton's birthday, and Clayton Clifton shot three robins with three shots. They were glad to see the robins back again because robins make better targets than the chickadees and chippies of winter.

As he goes out past Blackie and Princess, who are sitting at the kitchen table drinking a beer, Blackie takes his jackknife away from the carving he is doing in the linoleum on top of the table, and he gestures like a stabber. Blackie yells, "Get your ass out of here! Quit school, hey? Now you'll end up laid up like me with eight kids and The Welfare!"

"Sure sure," Clayton Clifton answers.

He walks up The Corner four houses away, sits on the stone wall smoking a Lucky, and he gives the hoot for Paulie Wilson to come out. Paulie, who lives in the house across from The Corner, hears, waves in the lighted window, and comes out, hunching his arms into his studded leather jacket.

"I'll get a jacket like that now I'll be working," Clayton Clifton says to Paulie.

It is too dark to go out shooting birds, and Paulie's brother is out in his new Willys with his girl from North Lake, so they can't go spotlighting deer, neither. Paulie's brother has a good job at the new pelletizing plant. The Company is open pit mining now the undergrounds have run out of high grade. The deer are moving out from the cedar swamps now the snow is almost gone, easy targets, starved and feeding next to the country two-ruts.

"Wanna light a grass fire?" Paulie says.

"We gotta get a six-pack first," Clayton Clifton says.

The boys comb back their beautiful hair, patting the side wings into perfect D.A.s, running their palms backwards over their heads with light touches, pulling on their sideburns, wiping the Vitalis on their jean legs. They start walking down the hill.

"Shit, wish we had a car," Paulie says.

"I'm going to get one soon's I start working," Clayton Clifton says. "A Jeep or a Chevy."

They begin to jog. Around the curves, the hill is a long one, lit by three dim lights, each a block from the others.

"Remember when we used to shoot these lights out with slingshots?" Clayton Clifton stoops to gather up a handful of small pebbles from the top of the cold tar. He throws them, one by one, at the middle streetlight, halfway down the hill. It is only a high-powered light bulb with a corrugated tin guard above it, easy to hit. Paulie begins to throw pebbles, too, from the downhill side. Soon one hits home, and the light goes out.

"Let's hide and scare people," Clayton Clifton says. The boys jump over the wall and crouch among the cedar trees in the black shadows, next to the remnants of the last snowbank, crusted and dirty, unmelted because the sun never gets to this side of the street.

"Move your ass, I'm getting wet knees," Paulie whispers.

"Shit, I'm just as wet as you," Clayton Clifton says. "Shhhh! I hear someone coming!"

But it is only Mr. Wiitala, staggering and weaving up the hill, getting home a little late from his work at Makinen's Paint Shop. No fun scaring a drunk.

They wait, jostling and swearing at each other, smoking two cigarettes each. Then they hear voices from down the hill, and giggles.

"Shhh!"

It is Maxine and Hester. They'd know the voices anywhere, heard them all their lives. The girls are coming home from that freshman party, sissy stuff, a bunch of kids acting like clowns, probably ducked apples and shit like that. The two girls have stopped talking since they passed the light down below and saw this light was out. They are now whispering silhouettes, fingertips interlocked in fear of the dark street, which is as quiet as the cemetery. They are walking fast to get into the arc of safety from the light on top of the hill.

The boys poke each other and leap over the wall, shouting like the soldiers in the war movies at the Saturday afternoon shows, going over the top. "Whoooo-eee! Let's get Maxine and Hester!"

The girls screech, scream, break hands, and run. The boys

chase them, whooping, for a hundred yards, then stop, out of breath, laughing so hard they have to bend over.

They turn back down the hill, walk to the highway, then along it next to the hospital, past the Swedish church with its high steeple, past the high school behind its iron spiked fence, past the English church with bats in its belfry, to the front of the King's Bar. They lean on the outside, one boot heel each up on the black shiny tile, under the blue neon sign shaped like a cigarette, smoking.

Soon Heikki Donatello, who is twenty-one, and a friend of Paulie's and Clayton Clifton's older brothers, comes out. They get Heikki to buy them a six-pack at the grocery store next to the bar, and Heikki gives them a ride back up to The Corner. They sit on the Stone Wall.

Their neighborhood is the only one in town with stone walls, and they are proud of them. The walls were built by Mather the Mining King, from Cleveland, Ohio. Or rather, they were built by men from the old countries, the boys' grandfathers, when Mather built his mining-town estate in their neighborhood. It is called Mather Cottage, but to them it is a mansion.

Clayton Clifton's mother Princess is a maid at The Cottage, like his grandmother was when she came from Sweden. She works there when they need extra help, when all the big shots come to town to check out the mines to see if they're making enough money. It has a pool room that they call a billiard room, and a room with red plush couches where they smoke cigars and read books with leather bindings, and a room where there is nothing but clean sheets and towels and napkins that aren't paper, called the linen room. The boys and the other kids have peeked into the windows when no big shots are there. The caretaker sees them and comes out and yells at them while they are running away.

They drink two and a half beers each, stashing the last one in a big hole in the wall where a stone is loose. All the little kids leave secret messages in that hole; the boys used to too, but there are none there now.

They throw the empties into The Pit, an old mine shaft, filled up with water. The cans hit the mush ice. The pit stinks in the summer and The Company has fenced it all around so no one will fall in. Once Mr. Juhanen drove an old car down and they pushed it in. They say the pit is bottomless. The water is soupy and green. The bottom must be piled with crap by now, about a mile down there, where the bottom is if there is a bottom. The neighborhood kids used to wonder if a deep sea diver could go down and come out in China.

They walk back to The Corner and head up the bluff through the pines and over the rocks, slipping with their smooth soles on the pine needles. They walk sure-footed, though, even with the slipping, because they know the way in their sleep, blindfolded. This is their territory and they have played every inch of it, all their lives.

"Christ, will those firemen shit when they try to get up to the fire!" Paulie laughs at the thought. "They'll trip all over on these trails."

Clayton Clifton belches. He is out of shape from sitting around and screwing Carol all winter. "Christ, sure will," he says. "Remember when we used to guide those rockhounds from Alaska and Georgia and places like that, for a quarter?"

"Yeah, they sure were dumb, coming all that way just to get this hematite rock."

They climb higher, holding on to the trunks of pine trees to guide themselves. The pitch is running, and soon their hands are gummy. They gather sticks, feeling at the bases of the trees, as they go up.

"Remember the year they tried to pull hoses up here?" Paulie says.

Soon they emerge from the pines onto Hematite Bluff's grass fields. To the north the Northern Lights flame. "Good night for The Lights," Clayton Clifton says, stopping to light a cigarette, taking a deep breath, cold, fresh.

"Yeah. The town looks bigger, too, from here, all lit," Paulie says.

They hike higher through the snow-flattened dry grass, the glow of the town below them at their backs. The stars are bright

• *Grass Fires*

in a clear sky. They reach the summit and sit with their backs against an outcropping. "Christ, it's beautiful from up here, must be what it looks like from an airplane," Paulie says.

"I'm going to ride in an airplane someday," Clayton Clifton says. "Maybe go down to Detroit to see the Tigers, or Milwaukee to see the Braves."

"Sure, sure, fancy, aintcha?" Paulie says.

Clayton Clifton takes a fresh book of matches out of his back pocket. They check the wind with wet fingers, ritualists, though they know it is from the southwest. They gather loose, long dry grass, and they make a tangled pile. Then they teepee the pile with dry pine twigs from their pockets.

Clayton Clifton sets the match book on edge, lighting one match pulled out and stuck into the book sidewise. He places the matchbook a little to the outside of the teepee, but in the loose grass. By the time the pile lights, the boys will be gone. The match book will be burned, and there will be no evidence of arson, except for the black bluff, where greener grass will grow. The fire always stops at the rocks which edge the bluff. They have learned to light the bluff from their older brothers and sisters, who learned it from kids who are now grown-ups and won't admit they know how.

"Wonder how Blackie and Mr. Wiitala and Hester's dad and Maxine's dad and them used to do it, before there were book matches?" Paulie wonders.

The match lights and the boys run down the bluff, as surely as Indians. They sit on the wall at The Corner and wait, sharing the last beer. Hester walks past on her way home from Maxine's house. She has her hair in braids again. Hester's parents don't believe in funny papers and lipstick and stuff like that, because of the Apostolic Lutheran Church, so Hester always sneaks to Maxine's house before the dances to let her hair down and to put lipstick on.

"Hi, Hester," Clayton Clifton says. "Didn't you have long hair earlier?"

"Hi, Hester," Paulie says. "It's Spring Night."

"That was you guys who scared us!" Hester points. "We thought it was some of the little kids. Grow up! Boy, we sure were scared!" she says in a tone of voice to let the boys know they weren't successful.

"Hi, Hester," Paulie repeats. "It's Spring Night."

"Spring Night?" Hester looks up the dark bluff. "Really?" "Yup," Clayton Clifton says. "Nothin' to do, so we did it."

"I'm going to go get Maxine," Hester says, and runs back down the street.

By the time the fire trucks come, the grass on the bluff is aflame high above the town, though the kids can't see the flames, because they are on the rocky side. Someone has called in the alarm, and the firemen in long black rubber coats are running up this stony side, bumping into pine trees, tripping on outcroppings and on their charred brooms that they use to beat out grass fires.

There are ten kids, aged ten and above, sitting along the stone wall, kicking their heels against the stones, with four more teen-agers standing in the street in front of them. They glow in the red revolving light of the fire truck parked a little up from them. Some of the older boys are smoking cigarettes. None of the girls are.

The fire chief strides up and down along the row of kids. Occasionally curtains part in a lighted house down the street, and an adult form appears. No adults come out of the house, though.

"How long have you kids been sitting here?" the fire chief asks. "Did you see anyone come down the bluff?"

"No, and we've been here all night," Maxine answers.

There is laughter from the group.

"We've been playing. Kick the can, capture the flag, sardines, I-make-the-frying-pan-who-puts-the-egg-in? in The Pines." She gestures behind her shoulder to the dark stand of virgin white pines behind the kids sitting on the wall.

"We would have seen if anyone strange came into our neighborhood," Hank Lehtomaki says.

"Cleveland Location kids notice outsiders," Paulie's brother Matti says.

The fire chief swears a few times. "I'm from Salisbury Location myself."

Grass Fires

"Cleveland always beats Salisbury. Those Cousin Jacks," Clayton Clifton says. "You know Blackie Peterson? He's my dad. He was born in Salisbury but then they moved to Cleveland."

Salisbury Location is only a mile away, over the other bluff near Lake Angeline, but it is as if it is on a distant planet, in this town.

"Blackie? Yeah. Used to work the Mather C with him until I got laid up," the fire chief says. He pats his fat belly. "Back problems."

"Yeah, well he told me all them Cornish Cousin Jacks live in Salisbury got to be foremen because they could speak English, not because they were good miners," Clayton Clifton says.

"Yeah, but the Italians were the worse, my ma says," Hester, who is sitting demurely at the end of the line, says. "The Italians always liked the Finnish girls. My ma says they used to come to Cleveland and the Finnish boys would chase them."

"Hester, shat up," Clayton Clifton says.

"I was never a foreman. That's them rich people on Strawberry Hill," the fireman says. "But we Cornish make the best pasties," he says, slipping back to childhood arguments among ethnic groups. "Hey, cut it out," he said. "I'm asking you about the fire."

"Blackie told me Cleveland always beat Salisbury and we lit the best fires first in spring," Clayton Clifton says.

"Lit the best fires?" the fire chief says. "Now, you ain't confessin' you lit this fire, are you?" He gestures behind them to the bluff, well-aglow now, to the long profile of the hill, silhouetted in the smoky orange glow from the high flames on the town side.

"He meant the lightning," Maxine says. "Lightning always catches Hematite Bluff first."

"You, girl! You got a wise tongue," the fire chief says. "Who's your dad?"

Clayton Clifton jumps down from his place in the row and he walks over to Maxine. He leans his back onto her knees and spreads them, his arms over her legs. He feels her thighs clamp the sides of his chest. He presses his arms down around her thighs in reply.

Grass Fires •

"Don't mind her, she always talks funny," Clayton Clifton says. "Cleveland always was the best, is what she means."

The fire chief gets nowhere, like he always does. Clayton Clifton remembers Maxine's thighs.

●

Years later, when the Cleveland Location kids have become adults gone from the Upper Peninsula, only returning on vacations, Maxine is in the laundromat downtown. She is smoking a cigarette, leaning against the high folding table, with one eye on the clothes tumbling in the dryer, and one eye on the street outside. This laundromat used to be a small grocery store where the kids bought penny candy after school. But chains like A & P came into town during the boom years, and small grocery stores closed. Now A & P is closing, too.

Across the street, where the Salvation Army used to be, and where there is a rock-strewn vacant lot now, she sees a disheveled man with baggy pants and a black leather jacket with studs on it, haltingly walk by, swaying. He begins to fall forward in slow motion, then catches himself, so that he looks as if he is doing the touching-toes exercise. Then he finds his balance again and stumbles on. It is Clayton Clifton.

Maxine runs out of the laundromat, shouting, "Clay! Cliffs! Clayton Clifton!"

The man turns, squints toward the voice, as if he is trying to focus his eyes, though it is a cloudy day and only three in the afternoon.

"Clayton Clifton!" Maxine shouts again. Then she crosses over. "Clayton Clifton, how are you?"

"Maxine?" He stares at her, swaying. "Maxine. F'r chrissakes! What you doin' home? Last I heard you was in Wyoming!" He teeters back and forth, spittle coming from the side of his mouth. Then he stops swaying. He straightens and says deliberately and slowly, "Maxine. Let me buy you a beer."

• *Grass Fires*

"I've got clothes in the dryer. Wait a minute." She takes his hand and starts across the street with him.

"I'll drive us. I have a car," Maxine says. "Do you want to go to the Napoli?" She leans him against the hood of her station wagon. "Or somewhere for coffee?" She leaves him leaning there and runs in to the laundromat and piles damp clothes into her basket. She comes out.

Clayton Clifton has waited to reply. "Nah, Franco kicked me out of da Napoli. Can't never go back 'dere. Le's go to the Sunrise." The Sunrise is the bar where all the town drunks hang out.

By the time they get there Clayton Clifton has fallen asleep, so she drives them home instead. Princess comes out and helps her get Clayton Clifton into the house. He leans and stumbles up the sidewalk where Blackie used to switch his kids. He is a dead weight, and stinks.

"He's been on a bender for a week," Princess says. "Just when he finally got another job.

"It was that girl—Carol. Running off and marrying Beckwith Blake like that. Maxine, sure is good to see you, honey. How many kids you got now?"

"Good to see you too, Princess," Maxine says. She sees Clayton Clifton now, as he was, pegging green apples at her as she swings.

●

Beckwith Blake and Clayton Clifton are sitting down the slope of their barn roof, on the side towards Maxine's house. Their loud rooster won't stop crowing. Maxine is twisting around on the swing beneath the apple tree. She likes to make herself dizzy, so she twists the ropes up, again and again, unwinding, over and over. Clayton Clifton says, "You should drink a few beers, if you like to make yourself dizzy."

Maxine stops, planting her tennies firmly into the slanted

dirt of the backyard hill. She shakes her head like a labrador retriever shakes off water—with her whole body, right to her shivering tail, Clayton Clifton tells her.

"God says you shouldn't drink until you're twenty-one," she says.

"Is God in Michigan? In the U.P.? Does he make the law that says that?" Clayton Clifton says, leaning over to wipe the spit off Beckwith Blake's chin.

"Stop spitting, Blake!" Maxine says from long babysitting experience. And she winds herself up again.

"Abigail Nellie! Wendy Mamie!" yells a deep, harsh voice. Blackie's.

"They're up the sandpile in The Pines with Shirley playing," Maxine yells to him over the roof. She is babysitting her sister Shirley while her mother goes grocery shopping.

"They're up the sandpile with Shirley," Clayton Clifton says to Blackie, scrambling over the other edge of the roof to talk to him.

"Shit!" Blackie says. "Can't you stop that damn rooster? I'm going to chop his head off, he doesn't stop!" Maxine has felt that way herself, especially at sunrise in the summers, when that rooster won't stop. Blackie limps back into the house, banging the door to the shed behind him.

Clayton Clifton looks down at Maxine twisting. "Wanna take a walk in The Woods to Lake Angeline?"

"Yeah," says Beckwith Blake. "Wannago ta 'gine?"

Clayton Clifton says, "I meant Maxine and me, dummy." Clayton Clifton is fourteen, and has just begun to jack off. At first he didn't know what to do with it, but the older guys kept him up on things. He is the best beer-drinker, though. That gets respect. He has just had a couple of Dalton Murray's beers, and he is feelin' real good.

"Oh, let him come, hey?" Maxine says. "He likes The Woods."

Maxine sways in the swing. She is getting older too, and her nipples show swollen beneath her t-shirt. "I have to wait until my

Grass Fires

ma gets home, though," she says.

"Yeah. Well, hoot me when she gets home," Clayton Clifton says, though he knows the sound of their car well enough, a '54 Ford, the Jubilee Special, with braces on its teeth. He scrambles over the tar-paper roof to the edge of the other side, and he drops to the ground in a ski-jumper's crouch, just like old Joe Perrault and The Flying Finns, the Bietila Brothers from just down the street, made ski jump history, their skis are in the U.S. Ski Museum just the other side of town, they taught all the neighborhood boys, Clayton Clifton learned to ski jump before he learned to ski ride.

He goes across the sidewalk into the shed, and then to the kitchen, which smells of yeast and sweat. His mother bakes a lot of bread. He turns right, to the bathroom, pees—a good beer piss. Blackie and Princess are sitting at the kitchen table drinking a beer. Blackie is carving with his jackknife, designs on the linoleum top.

"Wanna beer?" Princess says, her eyes blinking from the cigarette smoke from the cigarette in her mouth.

"He's too young!" yells Mrs.-Mrs. from her chair in the front room, where she sits with her legs so fat they roll like foam over her shoes, water on the knee, they call it.

"Shat up, Ma!" Blackie says. "Wanna beer?" he says.

"Nah," Clayton Clifton replies.

He climbs back up the roof, sure in his ankle-tied black gym shoes. He wants to have motorcycle boots.

"Get some shoes, Clay Cliffs," Maxine says. "Everyone's wearin' white bucks now."

"I beat up kids who call me that, Maxine."

"How did someone born in an iron mining town get that simpy name?" Maxine says, winding herself up again. "You sound like some guy in a book from England."

Just then Maxine's mother pulls up.

"I'm going to Lake Angeline with Clayton Clifton and Beckwith Blake," Maxine yells to her mother, heading from the swing up the backyard hill to meet the boys who are heading on their side, to the gate their families hold mutually.

"Shirley's across the street at The Pines' sandpile with

Abigail Nellie and Wendy Mamie," she shouts to her mother.

They are puffing, walking through the gout weed on the overgrown trail to the maple stand. Maxine picks a handful of wild tiger lilies, with a few ferns, and she stashes them on a rock to pick up on the way back.

"Do you remember when Hank would get us boys and we'd chase you from the frog pond, you and Hester?" Clayton Clifton asks.

"Ish!" Maxine says.

They walk in silence for a few hundred yards. Then Clayton Clifton asks the question that has been on his mind. "Do you have any hairs growing?" as they pass into the white pine grove just before they'll burst to the grassy granite bluff overlooking Lake Angeline, another old mine pit.

Beckwith Blake says, "Yeah, I got some."

"He wasn't asking you," Maxine says, taking Beckwith Blake's right hand.

"Under your arms?" Clayton Clifton asks.

Maxine is silent. Then, "Yeah," shy, as she picks from just above their heads a white pine frond, rolling it in her fingers for the smell. "Two to a bunch and all together they make a peacock's tail," she says, fluffing the peacock tail onto Clayton Clifton's nose, flirting.

Clayton Clifton feels himself growing. He hopes she doesn't see it, she wouldn't know what it was, and he passes his hand back and forth once or twice in front of him as he jiggles in his walk, missing a step, as if he is adjusting his pants.

She doesn't.

"On your bottom?" Clayton Clifton asks the question.

"I'm getting a few long hairs on my bottom," Beckwith Blake says.

"I wasn't asking you," says Clayton Clifton, leaning across Maxine to brush Beckwith Blake's hair from his eyes.

"He wasn't asking you," Maxine says, wiping Blake's spit off his mouth, and then running ahead, taunting Clayton Clifton to come running after her. Clayton Clifton catches her and grabs her

• *Grass Fires*

hand. They walk hand in hand over to the cliffs above the water which rises up the shafts, one inch or two per year. Then they sit down and don't say a word until it is time to go back.

As they head back, they hear Blackie, checking. "Beckwith Blake! Clayton Clifton!" Even Blackie's voice sounds sweet and new from up here.

• • •

BLUEBERRY SEASON

The long wet grass yielded as if with surprise as she cut through it, its tangles never having been brushed by a human leg. Her walking shoes were wet by now, but white buck shoes are sturdy, and very good for walking in the woods; these had, for years, and didn't look to collapse now. The blueberry bucket, a plastic aqua gallon wash pail with a twisted coat hanger handle, had seen its years of service also, and had carried from these woods and fields many treasures, including her first *Boletus edulis*, which she had recognized after taking the mycology course last winter. When she brought the mushroom to class, the instructor and the rest of them had to give her the crown, the honor of having found the most edible field mushroom that month.

She walked through a stand of white birches and searched for the two trees that formed a sort of arch, where the path could be found. Few people came into the woods these days, too busy watching television, but the path was still there, reappearing after every winter as if by magic, for it wasn't a wide path, nor a well-travelled path, but it had been here ever since she had lived near these woods, forty years now since they had moved to town after working in the Navy Yard in Virginia during the War.

They said, though, that the path the people on the Oregon Trail had taken with their covered wagons, was still visible on the prairies of South Dakota, even after the harsh winds and weathers of Dakota winters for over a hundred years, so maybe woods and fields received paths much as rock or marble received a sculptor's chisel; even on alpine tundra, the path the Ute women and children used to take over the 12,000 foot mountain passes in Rocky Mountain National Park were still visible, and the weathering there had to be immensely severe. If you didn't know the path was here,

• *Blueberry Season*

between these two birches, you'd never see it from the field below. One winter, cross-country skiers had tied fluorescent plastic ribbons on the trees to mark the path, but they had tattered, and were gone now, and she was glad.

    As she ambled along the ridge she almost called for Greta, and had to stop herself from looking back or to the side for the sleek black creature, who would be ranging by now, exploring animal holes and dens, but Greta was most likely dead by now. Eight months since she had disappeared into a Christmas eve snowstorm down at her daughter's place in Lower Michigan, and people kept saying that dogs have a homing instinct and appear on the doorstep after months, or even years, but she felt the dog to be dead, a black Labrador velvet lump frozen in some snowbank next to I-75, and she couldn't imagine how the dog would get across the Mackinac Bridge without having someone notice; she had told the people at the Bridge to be on the lookout for a female Lab when she had crossed back after the holidays, and nothing had been heard.

    "Greta?" she said out loud when the image got too strong, or the memory. Her voice was rarely used these days, except to talk to the mailman or to the neighbor down the road, or to a friend on the telephone, or to sing in church. She thought about her voice over the years, how it had been used in crying, laughing, soothing, yelling, cooing, gasping. Such a good thing, a voice, and so taken for granted, as she knew that she could speak if she wanted to, even if it had now been two days since she had used it, to answer a wrong number on the telephone. Her daughters and son chided her, told her to get another dog, to have a person come and live in; after all, you're getting older now, Mother; but she'd said, I've had animals—pets, children, people living with me—all my life, and I want to see if I can live alone with my own self. Loneliness isn't the worst thing in the world, you know. Just to see whether her voice would still do it, she let out her Tarzan yell, the one that she used to amuse the grandchildren. Fine. That voice worked fine.

    Still, it would be good to have a dog—Greta—a pet—as a companion, especially on these walks in the woods. Last year Greta had turned fierce and had dashed into the underbrush after something—a bear?—right around here, just about this time, blueberry season, though she'd never seen a bear out here. The newspaper said just the other day that the bears were coming out of the woods into the towns; several had been sighted outside Marquette, because this was such a bad year for blueberries, not enough rain in July, and too much in June. Well, we'll see, she said to her old aqua blueberry pail. We'll see if our secret spot has any berries.

Mother, her daughters have said, leave a note when you go out for a walk in the woods, so people will know, at least, which woods you're in, and she had said, who'd find the note? Nobody would miss me for days, and by then it'll probably be too late, anyway. But Mother, you could sprain an ankle, or break an arm, climbing up those rugged hills—or fall over a log, or drown in a lake, anything could happen to you, and who'd know? I don't know, she'd said; I'll have to take the risk, and she remembered herself on the ridiculous bicycle again, learning how to ride a bike at fifty, imagine, when she'd taken the pickup out to a country road, one lane paved in blacktop, and had put the bike in the back, so she could practice.

When she was young, she'd never learned how to ride a bike, and so she'd gotten on it, wobbling but going, finally going, and the blacktop was being eaten up in front of her eyes, peddling so fast as she was, and then there'd been the hill and the curve, going down that hill so fast, and the bicycle had gone right over the edge on the curve, and she'd tumbled down into the ditch, and got scratches and bruises, and a twig had pierced her right cheek, near her eye, so she was bleeding pretty much, too. This was before Norm died, and when she finally got home, the beat-up bike and the beat-up woman in that old clunker of a pick-up, he'd shrugged and asked her, just like the kids. Why do you go into the woods alone? Something is crazy about you.

Why indeed? Her thighs were brushing ferns now, a soft caress of bright green ferns, almost waist high in places, with soft honeydew grass, the slight click of stiff aspen leaves in the slender breeze, the smell of balsam, and her seasoned feet, sure on the foot-

Blueberry Season

wide path.

Down from the grove of birches and ferns, into a swamp, with black mud spongy, but not sinking wet, and the slap of high swamp bushes against her whole body, she performed her late summer ritual. She used her arms like a swimmer's, to break through, the path faint but still there, winding a little to take advantage of the least-wet terrain, and the hum of mosquitoes came after her, as she stooped to tie her shoe, warning her to keep moving or they'd pounce, attracted to her sweating now, in this moist ravine. Then to another small bluff, scrambling up and across a large exposed granite rock face that slanted down into the swampy place she'd just left. She wiped the sweat from her forehead with her sleeve, drying her hands on her jeans, setting the blueberry pail down for a minute while she caught her breath.

Apple trees grew here on this mound, the fruit green and small yet; sour, too. Her mouth reverberated inside when she tried a bite: another few trips here in the fall, though, when they would be ripe and crisp, would give her enough apples for canning applesauce and apple butter for gifts; she'd need a new food mill this fall, because she'd lost the spring on the screw of the old one, and the man at the hardware store downtown said it was so old they couldn't order a spare screw or spring. He said the new one would cost about $20.00, and she had to decide, is it worth it? Could she afford it, with heating prices the way they were, and the electric company just raising the rates again; she couldn't afford to get new insulation for the drafty old house, either; paying the heating bills would be cheaper; for how long? But she wasn't going to live many more years, she supposed, and she wanted to manage on what she had, even though the company had cut down her pension. They cut widows' benefits when the widows turn seventy. Well, maybe, she'd have to make applesauce the old way, peel the apples and core them, and mash them with the potato masher, white applesauce, even though the russet color of the food mill applesauce pleased her so, and was healthier. Well, it was a decision to be saved for later. For now, blueberries.

Her eyes turned downward, ground bound, scanning the

grade and the grasses and the bushes on this mound of rock and birch and apple trees, looking for a patch. There, on the reindeer moss, the small bushes she sought. Crouching, she saw the clusters of blueberries, tiny as a doll's pearl necklace, and her practiced fingers went to work. The patch of bushes had so many berries, she finally had to just sit down, picking within her arms' lengths, crushing the moss with her bottom, feeling the dampness filter through her jeans and underpants.

The gathering of August, this was, performed by her grandmothers in Finland, and then here in this land, the women going out to gather the berries. When she was a girl, they'd all go out picking, her mother and her sisters and her aunts, and then the children had to clean them. She'd sat under a tree with a huge galvanized laundry tub full of blueberries, and she and Laina would have to pick out the leaves and the twigs and the raw berries, careful not to crush the ripe ones; they would start cleaning them in the afternoon, after everyone had picked since early morning, breaking through dew, and the cleaning lasted under that tree, until dark set in. Now her own daughters and granddaughters lived in cities with malls and freeways, and they couldn't pick blueberries, nor clean them, but they could buy them at the supermarket, awful domestic berries that grew on high bushes and tasted like mush.

Her fingers worked in a plucking motion, gently, and she separated the ripe ones from the green ones by just the right amount of pressure, glad to have the use of her fingers still, for such delicate work; Norm's mother had had arthritis near the end, and had been angry when she couldn't pick the berries anymore; she saw the old woman, queenly in the middle of a burnt-over scrub pine blueberry field, sitting in a patch and feeding blueberries to her youngest grandchild, chuckling at the greed of the blue-faced boy. Mumuu was dead now. Concentrating so much on the picking, she barely noticed when the sound of the berries dropping into the pail turned from the drumming plop, the quick dull sound of berries hitting the bottom of a pail, to the silence of the second and third layers, berries hitting berries.

Four cups for a blueberry pie, one cup for blueberry muffins; she

• *Blueberry Season*

used to make her children pick one cup each, at least, when they'd go blueberry picking as a family, and she'd tell them that if they ate the berries they picked, no pie, no muffins; they had to save at least one cup each, and could eat the rest; they'd pick up their cups and then go to the car and beep the horn for her and Norm, just sit in the car with the mosquitoes and black flies, beeping to the wilderness, while she and Norm continued to pick.

That was when the children had hated blueberry picking, the stage every child goes through until the picking becomes a happy annual ritual. She had disciplined herself to eat only a few, just to whet her taste, but it was harder for the children; her granddaughter, when they'd come here a few years ago to this secret patch, had eaten every last berry she'd picked—Grandma, they're so good! Mmm! She smiled and popped a few berries into her mouth, rolling them around on her tongue before biting. If she came out here enough times, maybe she'd have enough for canning; nothing like blueberries in the middle of the winter, as a side dish with the thin Finnish pancakes she made herself for Sunday breakfast, royal purple in the snow.

Wandering from patch to patch, the next one under some cedar trees, the next in long grass where she could barely see the berries; and then there was the one in the cracks of the gray face of rock, and she sat on a crust of lichens, the pail half filled, enough for a batch of blueberry jam at least, even if she stopped picking now, which she wasn't about to do. A full pail or nothing. She wondered what time it was, and looked at the sun, but it had turned cloudy without her noticing it, so intent had she been. She had no idea which direction the sun was in; everything in the sky was gray-white, and she couldn't get a bearing on north or south, east or west.

She reached into her jacket pocket for the compass; never go into the woods without your compass, Mother, and a whistle, too, her son had said, and she had promised she wouldn't. She saw exactly where her compass was: right on the kitchen table, right next to her whistle, right where she'd left it when she went to the bathroom before leaving. Well, no matter; she knew her way around here blindfolded, she'd been here so much, and only a couple of miles from home, if you cut through the woods near the lake instead of taking the trail. Lots of daylight left; it looked to be about four in the afternoon by the amount of light in the gray sky, though she couldn't tell where the sun was. More patches of berries, and she wandered farther and farther, but closer to home, though, in an erratic semicircle. She had a feeling about these things.

In the middle of one patch, a black pile. Large and sausage shaped. Bear droppings? Human? She tried to remember what bear dropping looked like; she could only remember deer droppings, and rabbit, and fox. She shrugged, loosening her stiff shoulders, pausing from her picking to listen to the wind, to be quiet and receiving, to watch the chickadees on a nearby spruce as they scolded a squirrel. Sometimes the commotion of thought gets in the way of receptive observation.

She bent her head to avoid hitting a low branch, turned along a rock cut, and found herself in a wild raspberry patch. There is nothing so fragile as wild raspberries; the globules separated and fell into her palm, miniatures on an elf's plate; she had to be even more deft than with the blueberries, in order to pick the raspberries whole, but her fingers soon remembered, and quickly loosened the berries from the stem, and now she had a layer of raspberries on top of the blueberries. A sugar plum tree had some ripe, reddish-purple fruit, also, and so she put a few sugar plums into the bucket too, but even more into her mouth. This feast of wild fruit, with a few chokecherries for cleaning her palate, and they wondered why she spent so much time in the woods? Her fingers were quite stained by now, red and deep purple, and she licked them and wiped them on her jeans.

They say you can smell a bear before you see him, that he smells like a horse barn.

Farther into the raspberry patch, more droppings and a long oval of trampled grass, as if a creature had slept here. She had been so quiet in her luxuriating over raspberry treasure, and the wind was blowing into her face, so her smell wasn't that obvious.

• Blueberry Season

She was not really surprised when she met him.

They were right about the smell; it was awful, worse than any horse barn. The creature was up on the rock face, about twenty-five feet away, and it looked as startled as she when their eyes met, and held. "Black bear, range northern United States and Canada, 5 feet tall, 300 pounds, can run as fast as 25 miles per hour; worshipped by ancient northern primitive tribes as a life-giver. A constellation in the sky was named after a great bear. Bears were taunted by cowards in the city square, caged and made to earn their living by dancing with chains around their ankles."

Her mind snapped from reverie to fear and back again, as she stared unblinkingly at the dark brown bear with matted fur hung with thistles and burrs, and in her mind she saw him running across a slanted northern meadow in a fast lope, through birches and pines, crossing his territory; standing on the shore of a stream tipped on a large flat rock, waiting for trout; nosing into garbage cans and ripping tents; being captured and shot with tranquilizers and released in wilder wilderness by game wardens so it could recapture its former respect.

Motionless, their eyes held each other's for—forever—and they were entranced as lovers who meet at the airport after not having seen each other for a long time. She stood still, as loosely poised as a dancer preparing for adagio, and then she swept her arm towards him slowly, hissing softly in the back of her teeth while he stood above her on the high precipice of gray rock, looking down at her from the angled perch, while she offered this ancient, primeval memory her aqua plastic bucket of berries. She was surprised to know that she was not afraid of him. Still hissing softly, she held his eyes and then set the bucket on a bed of moss; then she backed up slowly, still holding his eyes. When he turned and glided in a smooth gallop, up the rock face and away into the cedar stand, she almost wept. She had not meant to frighten him out of his place, but it was her place, also.

She waited, motionless, for a very long time, hoping he would come back and eat her berries. But he didn't. Soon she wondered whether he had even ever really been here, or whether she had

Blueberry Season •

conjured him, imagined him from her need for company, whether she had summoned him by legerdemain, by her tribal deftness with berries.

The bucket seemed very heavy as she made her way in the direction she assumed was home; she had lost the place of the path. She who had been so blasé and confident, now stumbled and had to slide down steep hills, smashing through stands of ground pine undisturbed by bear or woman, and through swamps of cattails and through fields of blue harebells and into tansy that seemed to grab at her ankles with its stink that would bring an abortion to a girl who drank its tea. She felt tears.

She missed the bear. She wanted to touch him and comb his hair. Her daughter had called her up again last month and told her to get a pet, this show on tv said you shrivel up without touch, Mother, you need to touch and be touched, and she had been so blithe, hadn't she? in replying, I touch the trees, I touch the grass, I touch the plants and the berries, as if her daughter's suggestion were a joke. But now she knew it wasn't and she longed for a bear. She was unable to find the path home. In one of the cedar swamps she plowed through, she saw a pile of dark feathers, raven feathers from their size, but no bird entrails. No bones, no guts. Just feathers, a bird caught by a fox or a skunk and eaten up, just like that.

She was beginning to plan to spend the night in the woods when, as it got almost dark, she finally recognized a familiar crook of maple tree, over on the next bluff, to her left. Yes, she had been on target again, her instinct for home, her internal compass, right again, a woman of the woods hypnotized by a bear. It was dark by the time she got home, and she looked up the bear in the encyclopedia and then almost forgot him out there in her woods, as she sat in her warm yellow kitchen, cleaning the berries, smelling the muffins that baked in her oven, listening to a clarinet concerto on the radio.

• • •

• *Blueberry Season*

HELVI'S SAUNA

The cousins take off their shoes and hide them in Aunt Helvi's closet, next to her quilted satin bedroom slippers. "Shhh!" he may be up there," Arnold says, peeking around the corner of the stairwell.

"Nah, he's gone get drunk at Pestrollo's Bar again," says Marvin, who is thirteen, the oldest cousin still living in town. At ten, Maxine believes Marvin because he knows all about the secret places and about the family. Aunt Helvi says Marvin takes after Grandpa Millimaki, who died in the Depression, with skin cancer from the damp mines. "Just like our father, a real leader," Aunt Helvi says of Marvin.

The cousins creep up the narrow steps curving into the attic where Uncle Toivo lives, their wool-stockinged feet slipping on the clean gray painted steps. There are no rubber foot grips, and the steps are steep. "But he'll fall down these steps sometime when he's drunk," Marvin says. They get to the top and, sitting on the last two steps, Marvin looks around to the left, into Toivo's room. The children can smell the stale smoke. "He's gone," Marvin whispers.

The cousins scramble up the rest of the way. Five children enter Toivo's room. Just like last week, there lies the pile of dirty underwear in the corner. Just like last week, there lie the magazines with pictures of bare-naked women in them, scattered about on top of the rumpled bed. Just like last week, there lie the jumboes of beer, empty, their caps in the ashtray overflowing with Camel butts.

"Look at that big nail!" says Lila, the youngest on the expedition. "Dummy, that's a railroad spike," says Arnold. "Toivo works for the Section. He drives those spikes into the railroad tracks with a big huge sledge hammer."

Downstairs again, Aunt Helvi gathers the girl cousins for sauna with her. Maxine's father and mother go by themselves nowadays, since Maxine's younger brother looked too long at Maxine's mother's hair. Maxine herself stared at her father too long when she was eight, and from then on, she has joined the girl cousins on sauna Saturday. Aunt Helvi takes them, usually, but sometimes they go with Liisa, the old maid down the street who comes over each week to take her bath.

The four girls and Aunt Helvi sit on the benches waiting to sweat up, tossing water on the rocks so the steam sizzles on the round stones and up through the sauna room. "It's too hot!" yelps one of the younger girls. "Chicken!" someone replies.

"Sit on the lowest step," says Aunt Helvi, always the teacher. "Or crouch on the floor. Put a washcloth with cool water on your face."

"Bet you can't take it as hot as I can," says Maxine's cousin Sarah, issuing her weekly challenge.

"Bet I can," Maxine answers. "You have to climb up here, though, or it's not fair."

"Wait until I'm done, girls," says Aunt Helvi. "I can't take it as hot as I used to when I was young and on the go all the time. The girls—your aunts—and I used to have contests, too, to see which Millimaki sister could take it the hottest, but I never won."

They soap themselves, giggling and bantering, feet in buckets, rinsing by splashing water in washcloths over each other; then they throw more water on the rocks, and sweat up again, four slippery little girls and their plump aunt in a white plastic shower cap, slapping each others' shoulders with birch twigs. Finally they pour buckets of cool water over their heads for the last rinse. Sarah wins the contest because Maxine wants to get upstairs to see what the cousins will do next.

They dry off in the changing room, putting on the clean cotton underpants and long-sleeved cotton undershirts their mothers have packed for them in each family's sauna bag, those duffle bags piled with fresh scratchy towels smelling like outside from clothesline

• *Helvi's Sauna*

drying, with extra cakes of pine soap and round cardboard boxes of sweet-smelling powder topped with huge fluffy pink or yellow puffs, with extra boxer shorts for the fathers and extra shower caps for the teenage girls who don't want to get their hair wet because they have to go to the Youth Center dance or to a game later on.

Upstairs, pink and shiny-faced, with wet, slick hair, those of the family who have taken sauna already gather around the table in the eating kitchen. The grown-ups are drinking egg coffee and eating fresh cardamom rolls one of the aunts brought. There is strawberry pop for the kids. They take big handfuls of the cold cuts and make sandwiches on Finnish rye bread baked by Aunt Helvi and Grandma that morning. "I can make a bigger Dagwood than you," says Sarah. "Sure, anyone can," says Maxine, "but can you eat it? Aunt Helvi says we have to eat everything we take 'cause wasting food is a sin what with all the starving children."

Uncle Toivo has come home by now. He is drunk, as he is every Saturday night. Maxine can see him outside, his pants bagging, his knees bent, his fist raised like a saluter's in the war movies, gesturing. They can hear him yelling at Uncle Paavo, who is shoveling snow, how Uncle Paavo is a crumbum, never did nothing, hid the car keys when they were kids and wouldn't let Toivo use his car, always after the money, thinks he's a big shot now he works in the furniture store and not underground.

Last Saturday Uncle Toivo had yelled at Maxine's father, he should have stayed underground in the mines instead of letting them promote him to foreman, that's all you're after, money, think you're a big shot now, hey? Uncle Toivo has a memory long as an elephant's and he never lets his brothers and sisters forget when they did him wrong. Every Saturday night he picks someone for a shout but they never shout back, though they look mad sometimes, as if Toivo is a little child having a temper tantrum, or as if they're scared he'll punch them. Some of the uncles, married to the Millimaki sisters, and son-in-laws, don't know how to talk to Uncle Toivo at all, and just laugh tolerantly or angrily when he starts in with his picking and yelling. He has the gift of finding prick points in people and then jabbing and jabbing.

Helvi's Sauna •

The uncles go down for another sauna, together, with jumbos. Their wives sit in the living room on upholstered chairs in the warm light of the fringed lamps, and talk. Grandma, large and fat, sits near the lamp with the sewing stuff in compartments beneath its table, in the horsehair rocker, large and fat, laughing at all the little kids running, telling them "Don' don'!" as they run by, rattling the china cabinet where the dishes only used when ministers would pay their Sunday calls, rest in elegant china stacks behind the glass. Maxine has never seen anyone use those dishes, not even when the whole family is together for a wedding or a baptism.

The mothers talk quietly about each others' kids, and they smile a lot, and Grandma grabs a squirmy child running by, to give him "nooka," the eskimo kiss of rubbing noses. "Gimme to nose," she says, chuckling deep in her throat. "Gimme nooka." And the child reluctantly rubs noses with Grandma, for he would rather play than kiss. He smells her clean skin, rosy and nearly unwrinkled, even though she is seventy. Maxine has never had a real conversation with Grandma, because even though Grandma has been here in the Upper Peninsula for almost fifty years, she can't speak English, and Maxine's parents have never taught them Finnish, maybe because of the shame they themselves had felt when they entered school and had to endure the taunts of the other kids, who could speak English. Teachers arbitrarily gave English names to the children who couldn't speak, and were very firm that English be used. "Finn kids can't talk right," the kids used to yell. Of course, they yelled the same thing to the Italian kids, whose parents had emigrated there, at about the same time as the Finns.

So the women talk in English to each other, and in Finnish to their parents, and to their spouses when they want to tell secrets. The women seemed happy, chatting there softly, glad to be together there with the family, in this living room yellow and dim, as warm and inviting as fireplaces at ski lodges, as comforting as rocking chairs and hand-knitted mufflers.

Marvin leads the older cousins on a daring raid. They sneak through the dark damp of the basement, skittering across the clotheswashing room, into the Cold Room, where they used to

• *Helvi's Sauna*

keep the milk, and where there is often some kalia, a fermented yeast drink made in mason jars. Maxine's father had told her that in the old days, when he was a child, the room was always filled with water, and he had to wear big rubber boots to get the milk cans which he would deliver to people before he went to school. He told her some rich kids at the high school would laugh at him because he wore those big rubber swampers.

"Shhh!" Marvin warns, checking around the corner into the darkness. "They're in the changing room, I can hear them!"

The children scamper into the furnace room and spread about behind the huge furnace, as round as a redwood, with its monster arms reaching up to the ceiling. Marvin motions them on. Tiptoeing, they shuffle into the wood room, where the smell of the woodpile for the sauna stove envelops them. It is like being in a brand new house, thinks Maxine, like the one the uncles—except for Toivo, who always feels sick—and her father, are helping Uncle Heikki build on Sundays. The children turn the corner, flattening themselves against the cold cement walls, inching along, like the French Underground.

There, through the half-open doorway, sit seven naked men, with wet, slick hair and pink skin, lined up on the orange bench against the whitewashed wall of the changing room, their heads bent forward above arms resting on their spread legs, their things hanging down loose. Maxine closes her eyes hard. She wouldn't want Marvin and the cousins spying on her at sauna, seeing her nipples or anything. But she never forgets that picture snapped before she shut her eyes, and she remembers, too, that Uncle Toivo had finally stopped yelling at his family, there, taking a sauna with his brothers and brothers-in-law, taking a bath together, drinking jumboes together.

At home, as on every Saturday night, with the streetlight making the icicles at the window look like the entrance to a crystal cave, Maxine and her sisters say their prayers, "Our father who art in heaven; forgive us our trespasses as we forgive those"; while their mother listens. Then, with the three C's, as their mother calls them, Clean body, Clean pajamas, Clean sheets, crisp and windblown, Maxine sleeps the sleep of Saturday night, dreamlessly, forgiven.

Uncle Toivo grabs his fork with his whole hand, underhanded, and he bends his head down to six inches from the plate. He moves his mashed potatoes, turnips, turkey, dressing, salad, green beans, and cranberry sauce into a pile, smashes them so the mashed potatoes run red with cranberry juice and the salad runs tan with gravy, and he crushes two pieces of Finnish rye in his other hand. He slurps the food into his mouth very rapidly, pushing with the bread, leaning his bent head sideways so his greasy hair almost touches the plate, rolling his eyes toward the speaker.

"Right, right! You betcha!" with the food running down onto his shirt, dampening his belly with stains and splashes.

Sometimes he sits up to chew a particularly difficult morsel, with his mouth open, masticating loudly, smacking until he swallows it. Then down with the head for another bout of shoveling. He wipes his mouth on his tie during dinner, ignoring the napkin next to his plate. Usually he doesn't wear a tie, though, and he wipes his mouth on his sleeve.

Maxine and her sister have set the table. Then, when everyone is moving to take seats there, they watch where Uncle Toivo sits, and take the seats farthest from him, on the same side as he, so they won't have to watch him chewing with his mouth open and talking at the same time. Maxine and her sister complained about Toivo's table manners once to their father, but their father said they shouldn't talk that way about their uncle. Maxine's mother said she's noticed it too, but after all, this is a holiday, and God said we should love everyone, especially our own family.

"Didn't the minister preach a nice sermon?" Aunt Helvi says, dabbing the side of her mouth with the corner of her white linen napkin. "I always like sermons about Sisu and how the Finns have it."

"I am getting so sick of hearing about Sisu," says Maxine's sister. "Why doesn't he preach from the Bible, like other ministers?"

"Now, girls," Aunt Helvi says. "You need to know about

• Helvi's Sauna

your heritage and about the Winter War and how the Finns beat the Russians and fooled them on their white skis with white outfits on, and how the Finns are the only ones bordering Russia who aren't communists, and about Sibelius and Saarinen and how we really have gumption and are stubborn and about Lemminkainen in the *Kalevala* being born out of the ocean and establishing the land of heroes from a tiny oak seed and the love of the maiden Siirila, or was that Heskimoinen, I never can keep his name straight? Didn't the choir sound nice?" she continues, turning her head to look at Maxine. "Your cousin Helen is always such a good singer. But of course we Millimakis have always been musical. I wonder why you didn't join the choir this year, Maxine? Too much to do in school, I suppose. When I was teaching junior high I used to give homework, but not like nowadays. Of course I only teach second grade now, but a person has to move where her husband goes, doesn't she? We Millimaki women take care of our men, don't we?"

Maxine nods, Maxine's father and mother nod, Maxine's younger brother and older sister nod. Aunt Helvi was always a great talker. But a heart of gold, they all say, so everyone listens. Aunt Helvi is the family historian and she knows all sixty of her nieces and nephews and what grades they are in, and no matter what their last names are now, she always calls them Millimakis.

"That's a nice hat, Helvi," Maxine's mother says.

"Do you like it? I got it at J.C. Penney's for $6.59. That's dear for a hat but I do like blue velvet. My ex—" She sighs. "My ex used to say he liked me in royal blue, like a queen, he would say. But of course my hair was white prematurely and blue and white are the school colors and they always look good. Now with just Toivo at home and he doesn't notice anything—." She gestures to Toivo, who is busy eating.

"Right! Right! You betcha!" he replies, his mouth full.

She continues. "I got a letter from Esther last week. Your cousin Tessa is going to get a scholarship for college, she's going to study domestic science at the Normal and be a teacher."

Aunt Helvi still calls the state college, that is now called a "university," "the Normal School."

"Of course, Tessa was always one of the smartest Millimakis, just like you, Maxine, she reminds me of our mother. Mother only went to second grade, then she immigrated and was a cleaning lady, can you imagine that, so young? She worked for the mine bosses, but when they had the milk business she kept all the books in her head, just like a steel trap, she knows her math. Mother wanted to come for dinner, too, but she gets too tired, these diabetics have to watch everything they eat."

Helvi pauses for a breath and a sip of coffee. Everyone sits around the table dumbly nodding their heads at her torrents of words.

●

"Aunt Helvi is getting divorced," Marvin tells Maxine. "We can't call Uncle Edward 'Uncle' anymore."

Maxine is eight, just getting to the age when girls start sitting down and listening to their mothers and aunts talk. The women talk for hours at sauna about Edward and Helvi.

"Edward was stepping out with that Italian woman who sells the liquor in his grocery store."

"Mother, what is 'stepping out'?"

"His family bosses Helvi around."

"She packed her bags right up and came here home to the family where we love her."

"No one in this family ever got a divorce."

"And her a schoolteacher, too. I say she should stick with him."

"Imagine, Edward, acting like that!"

"He never did go to church."

"The Finnish boys always liked the Italian girls. And they won't even set foot in a Lutheran church, you know."

"Never go out with a Catholic, girls. You have to give up your church."

"Helvi, you'll pull through. You're better off without such

• *Helvi's Sauna*

a man. You can take care of Grandma and Toivo."

"Unless Toivo finds himself a nice woman."

"Who'd marry him?"

•

"Here, Maxine. Take this envelope to the Laitinens on Jackpine Street, you know where they live?" Aunt Helvi says. "Mr. Laitinen was hurt in the mines and they have six kids, you go to school with their girl, don't you? Don't tell them who sent it."

Maxine puts the car into gear and drives Aunt Helvi to her bridge club. "It'll be good to see the girls again," Aunt Helvi says, adjusting her royal blue pillbox hat. "What with Mother in bed, and schoolteaching, I haven't had time to go out gallivanting. Pick me up at nine thirty now. A girl needs her beauty sleep." She chuckles. "And here's a dollar for gas."

Maxine drives to the Carnegie Public Library, where the kids are studying, and gets her girlfriend Susu and they go to the drugstore and have a tin roof sundae, which Maxine buys for them with her dollar.

Maxine and Susu walk down the sidewalk towards where the car is parked. Across the street, staggering out of the Sunrise Bar, comes Uncle Toivo. "Oh God, Susu! Don't let him see me! There's my uncle, the town drunk!" Maxine hides behind her friend until Uncle Toivo lurches around the corner. Maxine doesn't talk much to her friends about Uncle Toivo. She wants to pretend he doesn't exist.

"I have to go up to the Laitinens for a minute," Maxine says, as she guns the car up the hill in second gear, past the town's skyscrapers, the mine shafts, and then, in high, down Jackpine Street. "I'll be out in a minute."

"Mrs. Laitinen? This is for you," handing her the envelope. Mrs. Laitinen looks puzzled, then opens it. Maxine can see Mr. Laitinen, his leg in a cast, watching Arthur Godfrey. TV is snowy again tonight, and she can hardly see the figures on the screen. It is 200 miles south to Green Bay, where the programs come from, and the signals aren't good, but almost everyone has a television set anyway. "How are you, Mr. Laitinen?" she asks.

"Frank! There's a hundred dollars here!"

"You're the Millimaki girl, aren't you? I went to school with your uncle. Why are you bringing us this money, though God knows we need it, him laid up and all."

"You know I play the organ? Well, the minister told me someone left it in the collection for you," Maxine lies. "So I told him I'd bring it to you." Maxine has told this lie before.

Maxine is cleaning house for Aunt Helvi one Saturday morning. Uncle Toivo, sober, comes up to her, puts his arm around her, asks her in his guttural voice, "Howshagoin', Maxine?" He fingers her bra, almost snaps it.

The next summer, when her cousin from Waukegan is visiting, she tells Maxine that she thinks Uncle Toivo snapped her bra. The cousin also tells Maxine about Uncle Toivo yelling and shouting, and about Aunt Helvi, how she cries at night when he is drunk. "He's like a crazy man! Do you think he beats up Aunt Helvi or anything?"

"No. They'd kick him out of the family if they ever found out he laid a hand on Aunt Helvi. She's just embarrassed to have you over visiting and you have to hear it. He yells at all the aunts and uncles, who aren't even his brothers and sisters. You know how Aunt Helvi wants everything to be nice? She's just ashamed about him, as if he's her husband and not her dumb brother that everyone in the family knows is like that."

Maxine has never wondered what it must be like, there in the family home, now that Grandma has died, with just Aunt Helvi and Uncle Toivo living there. She asks her father what he thinks about Uncle Toivo. Is he dangerous to Aunt Helvi? "Oh, he's a good boy when he's sober," Maxine's father says. "He's the black sheep, never finished school, so we have to take care of him, he had scarlet fever when he was a baby and was never right after. Helvi needs a man to take care of, now she's divorced. All the Millimaki

• Helvi's Sauna

women do, it's the best thing for her, taking care of Toivo."

Maxine doesn't tell him about the bra fingering

•

Maxine and her friends start going to certain bars to dance to rock and roll music and to drink beer. They have just turned twenty-one, finally legal. They go to the teacher's college as commuters and they live at home. Their fathers are miners, and they can't afford to go away to school. Sometimes her friends want to go to the sleazy bars, where the town drunks hang out, but Maxine never goes with them, because she thinks she might see Uncle Toivo. As it is, she looks all around in the bars they do go to, in case he might be there, and if she sees him slouched down over the bar with a cigarette and a long ash running over onto the bar, gesturing and talking to someone who seems embarrassed, she turns quickly and leaves before he sees her.

Marvin, whose father, along with Maxine's, is the only other brother left in town, now the underground mines have been closing down and all the workers have been moving to Detroit and Waukegan to get work in the auto plants, also comes to the bars to dance and to drink beer, but when he sees Uncle Toivo, he goes up to him, pats him on the back, and says, in imitation, "Howshagoin', Uncle Toivo?"

Marvin thinks Uncle Toivo is a joker and Marvin says Uncle Toivo used to let the best farts at sauna when he'd take the boys, like Aunt Helvi would take the girls. Maxine is disgusted. Marvin's younger brother got a dog last year and named it Toivo "because it eats like a slob and pisses all over," though they don't tell Toivo that. Toivo was very pleased at having a dog named after him, and he said he is going to leave all his money to Marvin's brother.

"What money?" Maxine asks. "Oh, he's a cagey one," says Marvin. "He only pays ten dollars a week to keep up the house and for food and everything, and Aunt Helvi pays the rest. Sometimes she asks him to pay more, but he says she's too big for her britches, these schoolteachers thinking they're better than everyone else, so he won't. He's got three insurance policies from Uncle Benny. What can they do? They can't kick him out, y'know."

Maxine asks her father if that is true. "Well, it could be. I know he makes good money on the Section. Helvi's never said anything to anyone, and even if she did, what could we do? We can't make him pay more if he doesn't want to, and we can't kick him out, he's our brother after all."

Maxine is sitting at a table, on a date with a boy she is trying to impress. She has her back to the door, which she almost never does.

"Maxine!" she hears the guttural voice yell. A large, bearlike figure staggers over to her through the smoke. "What you doin' here? This is a beer garden!" Maxine thinks now the jig is up. "I'm having a beer and dancing with my friends. Jack, this is my uncle, Toivo."

"How do you do, sir," Jack says, standing up and extending his hand. "Won't you join us?" Maxine silently wishes, "No!"

"Sure t'ing. Howshagoin'? Hot night, hey?" Toivo sits down. He starts to reach into his pants pocket, then has to stand up to do it because his pants are slung so low under his belly, and he pulls out a wet bill, folded and crumpled.

"Here, Maxine, it's a dollar," Toivo says, extending the traditional gift of uncles and aunts to nieces and nephews.

"Thanks, Uncle Toivo," Maxine says. "It's a twist, Chubby Checker. Excuse us, Uncle Toivo," she says, pulling Jack by the hand onto the dancing space. She keeps Jack out there twisting for three or four numbers, until she sees Toivo rise and lurch out of the bar.

The dollar bill smells of urine.

Maxine comes into the house the next Thursday to pick up Aunt Helvi for evening services, where all the grandmothers, the old Finnish ladies in their black wool overcoats and black hats go each week. When Maxine comes down the church basement to get Aunt Helvi, the ladies shake hands with her; their hands are

• Helvi's Sauna

translucent, and knobby from the hard work of their lifetimes. All the old ladies are widows, their husbands died from accidents in the woods or in the mines, or from heart attacks, cancers, and other premature causes.

Aunt Helvi says she likes to go with the old people "because these were Mother's friends, and besides, I can keep up on my Finnish. Church doesn't seem like church if it's in English." Maxine remembers it's been in English as long as she can remember; she herself can't even talk Finn, except to say Merry Christmas and hello and stuff like that.

When they get back, Maxine walks in to the house with Aunt Helvi to pick up her mother's cake pan. Uncle Toivo is sitting in Grandma's horsehair rocker, where Maxine has never seen anyone but Grandma dare to sit, with a jumbo in his hand. When he sees Maxine, he jumps up and starts pointing and yelling. He is drunk and not a good boy. "Helvi, I saw her in the beer garden. A nice Finnish girl with lipstick on and in tight pants, wiggling her hips!" He looms close, threatening, seems about to strike Maxine with his upraised fist.

Aunt Helvi yells at him, "Leave Maxine alone!" and she pushes Maxine out the door ahead of her. "That's all he's been able to talk about since last Saturday," Aunt Helvi says. "I told him he must be crazy, nice Millimaki girls don't go to beer gardens."

Maxine doesn't say anything; it would take too long to explain how times have changed, and she admires Aunt Helvi and loves her and doesn't want Aunt Helvi to be disappointed in her. Besides, Aunt Helvi is getting deaf, and it is difficult to talk to her for very long.

"Aren't you afraid of him, Aunt Helvi?" Maxine asks. "He's so strong, and so angry. Don't you worry he'll hurt you?"

"Oh no, when he gets like that I just go upstairs and close my bedroom door and put my earplugs in. He kicks for awhile but then he just falls asleep. And he's a good boy when he's sober."

•

Maxine and her mother are taking a sauna. It is Saturday night, and they are the only ones at sauna. They came over early to put the small logs into the sauna stove so the water and the room would get good and hot, since Uncle Toivo doesn't like to light the sauna anymore. Then, after supper, they come back over, passing through the room where all the aunts used to sit and chat, saying hello to Aunt Helvi, who is watching Lawrence Welk.

Aunt Helvi, now she's retired, doesn't go gallivanting anymore; she's afraid, and she seems to have lost the old spirit. Her legs are encased in brown support stockings, rolled down, her feet in worn flannel bedroom slippers. She is wearing a print housedress, and her hair is in curlers. Maxine has never seen Aunt Helvi in curlers before. Aunt Helvi says that Uncle Toivo is "gone to the store for some rolls," but Maxine and her mother recognize that for what it is. Uncle Toivo is downtown in the bars.

Maxine and her mother lean back on the top shelf with their legs up, talking and sharing confidences, as they always do in the sauna when Maxine, her husband, and their children come "home" from the city, on vacation. The two women have sweated and grimaced, putting washcloths soaked in cold water to their noses, throwing water from ladles onto the smooth rocks gathered decades ago from the shores of Lake Superior. "Bet I can take it hotter than you," Maxine says to her mother in the old challenge, knowing she can't; not a sauna regular like her mother, not a true Finn.

There, comfortable in the place where they'd always been able to tell their secrets, Maxine's mother tells her something. "Once I was down here alone on Saturday night," she says. "Your father was out of town on a job and you kids, you were out with your friends. I don't like to miss my sauna, so I came alone. It's sure different now that everyone, even you kids, has moved, remember when the whole family would get together on Saturday? Anyway, Uncle Toivo came down to use the toilet down here, it sounded like

• *Helvi's Sauna*

a waterfall, and then I heard him clearing his throat like he does, all those nonfiltered Camels, hocking and spitting, you know what I mean? Snorting?

"All of a sudden, there he was, right there in that doorway, silhouetted with the light in back of him, with his pants down. He was drunk and weaving. He looked at me up and down and said, 'The guys on the railroad think I have the biggest dick alive.'

"First I was just so scared. He's big, and he stroked my hip once, and when he's drunk he's violent. I covered myself as best I could. He took a step towards me. Then I just got so mad! The nerve! I told him go get himself out of here. Immediately! I told him I'd tell Daddy and the rest of them what he'd done and they'd kick him out of the family. He muttered, took a few steps toward me, and then he turned around and left."

"Did you tell Daddy?" Maxine asks, her skin starting to prickle more and not only from the heat of the sauna. She notices as if for the first time, her mother's beauty, her smooth white Finnish skin preserved by years of saunas, unwrinkled and pale, even alabaster, shining with sweat. She notices her mother's breasts, full, not sagging, with pale pink nipples. Together, she and her mother in the sauna are like Vuorenjuuri's painting of women at their bath.

"Oh no. I'd never do that. I don't know what Daddy would have done. Toivo always said, when he yelled at Daddy, that I was too good for Daddy and should have married him, Toivo, instead. Can you imagine? Besides, Toivo was drunk. Still, every time I come to sauna I make sure to hook all the doors, even that one, from the hallway where we bring the wood in. I had hooked the other one, but I forgot that one, and that's where he came from."

Years later, Maxine dreams a sauna dream. She is walking to Grandma's house. She turns the corner in a snowstorm and under the street light through the snow she can see a trail of vomit and urine, and marks from hands and knees. Drunk's tracks are not pretty, though the tracks are filling up with heavy snow by now. Maxine knows from the signs that her uncle has passed this way. She gets through the wind and wet snow to Grandma's house. She enters. She has come to beg Aunt Helvi to leave this ignorant drunk, even though he is her brother; why should a woman have more loyalty to a brother than to a husband? Uncle Toivo is sprawled in a faded purple easy chair. He greets Maxine loudly, starting across the room to her. She has begun to plead with Aunt Helvi to leave, to please, go out gallivanting again in your royal blue pill box hat, teach school, play bridge with the girls, go to church on Thursdays, send me with a hundred dollars to needy people.

"Howshagoin'?" he yells, slapping her back, feeling with his fingers for her bra strap, but she is a modern woman nowadays, and has given up wearing bras. Maxine is so revolted by him, by his smell, his fat belly, with his shirt out of his pants—his baggy, filthy pants with urine stains, held up at the level of the top of the crack in his rear by a twisted leather belt—that she puts her hand to her nose as she steps away from him. He is sputtering words she can't understand, his speech defect aggravated by the liquor. Aunt Helvi is sitting in her very neat print housedress, in thick support hose and wedgies, on the couch, telling him in an ever-louder deaf-person's voice to "Leave Maxine alone!"

Then he starts grabbing Maxine's shoulders. As he turns her to him she can feel how strong he is, the result of those years driving spikes, very big, very tall. She tries to pull away from him. He puts his face a foot from hers and pulls her chin towards his so she is forced to face him. Before she closes her eyes, she notices the beads of sweat on his forehead. His breath is rank, overpowering, cigarettes and booze and bad teeth. "You've always been pretty," he slobbers.

Aunt Helvi yells his name—"Toivo!"—and he turns to Helvi to yell obscenities, loosening his grip a little—but then, quickly, his hand drops, to slide down the front of Maxine's shirt and across to where her nipples are. She wrenches away from him. She bends over, with her hands crossed in front of her, screaming, "Go away!"

He pulls her up again, fast. His eyes move back and forth searching her shirt. Then he grasps her even tighter and pushes her hand down to his crotch where she can feel him, large, hard. She

• Helvi's Sauna

struggles to get away and he slaps her; then he grips her arms again, and she is powerless. She knows she will have bruises.

Aunt Helvi is now up and pulling at his shirt, telling him to leave Maxine alone. He mutters into Maxine's ear an invitation for her—"Love me," he says. "I'm in this family too," he says. And she screams NO and swears at him in the Finnish curse words she knows, but he is very strong and she is afraid he will beat her, rape her, kill her.

He drags her to the changing room of the sauna. Aunt Helvi is still struggling, her ankles turning on her wedgies, trying to pull him away from Maxine. The light here is bright, brighter than the TV light upstairs, from the one 100-watt bulb hung on a cord from the wooden ceiling. Helvi begs him to let Maxine go but he won't. She whispers in Maxine's ear as Maxine bends over in a faint. She says she has found the best way to stop him when he gets this way is to say he'll be kicked out of the family. Then he falls asleep in a minute or so.

Helvi sits down on the orange bench and starts taking off her support hose, showing her garters. Maxine yells, "If you don't stop, we'll kick you out of the family!"

This is the ultimate threat. He falls to his knees with tears in his eyes and keels over, falling asleep, snoring.

Maxine decides to take a sauna with Aunt Helvi for old times' sake. They step across him, enter the sauna room, and begin the purifying ritual. There are clean towels and new soap on the bench outside. There is nothing to say. All family secrets surface. They soap themselves silently, throwing more and more ladles of water onto the rocks, letting the steam do it, smacking themselves with birch branches tied in bundles.

•   •   •

POEMS

"The Gate: Cleveland Location"
Photo: Steve Navarre

WRITING POEMS IN A COLD COLD WORLD

Why does a person write poems when there's nobody out there to read them? I subscribe to several literary journals where poetry is published, and have a large collection of poetry books by contemporary writers, but I guess I'm unusual. Yet I'll wager there are few people who haven't been moved to write a poem in the throes of emotion—love, anger, sorrow. I asked a graduate class how many people read poetry for pleasure, and of the thirty teachers there, many of them English teachers, only two admitted to it. I know that when the poets on our campus give our annual reading, only a few people come unless the professors have assigned the students. I like to go to poetry readings because they remind me of worship. The air is filled with considered words, and when the artist, the fiction writer, essay writer, or poet, can savor and can express out loud in a dramatic fashion, these words—in other words, the writer has to be able to perform—I leave the reading with a feeling of spiritual awe. Perhaps the hard work required of the listener at such events is the reason people don't buy, read, or attend to poetry.

I have been writing poems for many years now— poetry is a natural means of expression. By this time, I know when I will (or will not) write a poem about something. I get an indefinable feeling of edginess, anxiety, that is only assuaged when I write. I work with pen in my journal, or on my computer, in line form. The fun of writing a poem is revising and revising, thinking, trying out, reading it out loud, singing it in rhythm, seeing whether it fits some urgent mental format that seems to arise through the writing. Writing poetry is an exercise in specificity. Finding just the right word, trying it out, counting its syllables, checking on its connotations, or seeing where it will lead the meaning, all provide great pleasure to me. I really don't write for the readers but to please myself, because I know I have few readers and will probably always have few readers. I write and revise as a form of seeing clearly and saying well. I am in a state of elation as I drive around trying out different words, running back and forth to the word processor to print out just one more version to see whether this one works. It may take years to get it so I don't want to revise it anymore.

Such a private, personal passion playing with poetry is! No chance of fame or fortune. The elite art, some people call it. You've read some of my poems inspired by various events in the essay, "My Writing Life," and here are some more considered words. Lately I've been having fun playing with sonnet form, and so you'll find a few here.

Postcard from Cedar Lake
NINE FEASTS
TOWARD SWIMMING

purple
    sugar plums picked off the trees
magenta
    chokecherries dry on the tongue
blue
    berries our warmup: we bend we stretch
tan
    mushrooms, puffballs, Boletus like buns
red
    jelly pin cherries tart and tiny
green
    apples pucker the cheeks
rose
    raspberries tumbling in grapebunch
orange
    poison mountain ash jubilee for the eyes
white
    peeping wintergreen minty smells fresh

dive dive dive into clear northern water
slime fronds from bottom tickle our toes
we burp foraged bounties
when swimming our lake

• *Nine Feasts*

LILAC TIME

for one week a year
the house smells
like old ladies
with too much perfume
a solid smell
it means business
tough
as an old maid schoolteacher
who rides camels
near the pyramids
during her summer vacation

WALKING TO CHURCH ON CHRISTMAS EVE
—to my mother

my mother and I walk
down the hill in boots
it snows just like expectations
the 11 pm service

I say I feel my failures
especially the divorce
she says "Failure?
Forgive yourself.
Everyone has failed."

we pass railroad tracks
where steam locomotives
used to pass with iron ore
no trains technologize
this sparkled eve
I say I feel my loneliness
she says, "Loneliness is not the
worst thing in the world."
we talk about
the pleasure of solitude

we live too far from each other
my children can't be here
I'm her only child who can

we walk by the hospital
where my father died
she says she has no more headaches
I say I've read

only the retarded are happy
she says, "And that's
doubtful too."

confession over
at church we sing
light a neighbor's candle
walk home silent midnight
snow comes down

she says,
"It looks like a Christmas card."
I say, "It is."

FROM A PORCH IN THE LES CHENEAUX ISLANDS
—to Carolyn

after long heat
and great stress
I drove through
a long corridor
chicory and Queen Anne's lace
daisies and goldenrod

emerged to this rocking chair
on a white and green porch
in a gentle morning rain
grey skies and slow boats
parched Ohio
verdant Upper Michigan

mallards *en famille*
glide along shore
sigh, signal
white water laps
to wind in cedars
with looping gulls

and last night!
I will never forget you
backlit by moon
beamed on the dock
our bare feet swung on edge
of still, black water

• Les Cheneaux Islands

I could have jumped
into that soft black
void or element
slipped breathless into
relief or joy
so glad was I to be here.

Les Cheneaux Islands •

Postcard from the Hill Street Trail
CROSSCOUNTRY: MICHIGAN
—to Susan

dry brown maple and oak leaves
rattle still on branches
the creak of saplings,
and silence.
our skis rasp when we fling
on this crusted snow
whir as we bend to hills
today the sky is colorado
and the lights ends on gray rocks
mountain ash berries on their branches
look like Christmas decorations
through bare trees
near dark green cedar swamps
squirrels that glance across the track
cross trail with snowshoe rabbits
passing by
the hats of acorns on the path.
on a sunny day we go in sweater
arms bare-headed and the snow
tinsels grainy with slices of ice.
we should have used red wax.
we go fast, we crabwalk up the hills
the shadows of twigs crisscross
a black and white oriental rug beneath us
shadows of the sides of the grooves
look like mountain ridges from a plain
and there is no rejection here
the ground receives the snow in lumps
soft and sculpted mounds
a casual overlay.
the grass insists near rocks and trees.

• *Crosscountry: Michigan*

young boys we pass gleam sweat
on lips and brows
but we are fit
we keep our sweaters on
and tramp beyond them.
we knew this place
before they made it public.
we stop to talk
about our lives
away from here
we lean on poles
face sun on slope
Susan,
it is good to be as we are
friends since we were three
in love with movement on skis
on snow in woods
we are this place's children
this healing is enough.

Crosscountry: Michigan •

SUNSET WITH GIRLS
—to Ruth and Bruce

"Come out!"
Mother strides in with her dog
"The sunset! We must go
up on the bluff to see it!"
Rachel, 3, calls
"Grandma, wait for me!"
Elizabeth, 8, calls for Erin.
Erin, 11, flounces out,
"I was reading a good book."
We follow Mother up
over roots and rocks
the familiar trail

we climb
in luminous dusk
cantaloupe watermelon sky
after the drought
the ground gulped
rain today
the earth smells horse

the swirl of large mosquitoes
follows us
we flail at them
bat with maple switches
climb past dark silhouettes
Norway and white pines
to the pink-orange top
finally we stand
panting on the crest

• Sunset With Girls

turn west

"Let's pick blueberries"
Elizabeth says.
"We're here to see the sunset."
"I saw it already," Rachel says.
"The clouds look like potatoes."
she lies down
on an outcropping of hematite
reclining, kicks her heels

the sun plunges in a dive
stunned in darkness
we stumble down
sweating from miracle
even our girls
seem to glow

IT SNOWED ALL NIGHT
—to Rebecca and Douglas

it snowed all night and light for two days straight
the hounds of heaven wailed and blew and yowled
we stayed inside, read books, made tea and ate
the third day, calmed, the snowplows walled
the roads; they sprinkled them with sand
brown sugar topping formed on Jasper Street
but back up in the woods on skis the fairyland
unfolded, pure, white, fallen, deep. No sleet.
Far crystals round the sun in pink aureole shone
through rapid clouds, the day a swan's wing, down
of goose, marshmallow pillow, Ivory flakes
We put our gaiters on, skied frozen lakes,
still ridges, decked with spruce and pine through
snowy tunnels, paths. Sweet, sweaty climb.

SONG FOR A MIDNIGHT SWIM

The languid boil of water in the sauna stove
soft jazz, a lamp, a moon rise on the lake
sweat drips, steam lifts from my nude body
lashed with woven imprints of the chair.
I put on old blue shoes and naked sprint the hill,
jump into cold black water. Ooof!
such mist is part of me, a time exposure slow
to cool to water temperature. Finnish loaf
and tea await. The whites of my bent legs glow
crouched on pebbles. Woodsmoke incense pervades air.
A bat swoops low for insects.   Shadows bark
in silhouette, beg, whimper,
       wait for me to come to light.
"Come in to warmth from dark."
I trudge uphill. My friend the water sets me free
My frosty forebears smile to guard me here.

THE BAPTISM
—to Denise and Ralph

In 1991, my daughter called
"I've found my love. He's coming north with me
for Grandma's 75th surprise birthday
we'll be there at 3."
The family, gathered there to celebrate
looked hard at Ralph, Italian kid
from Bensonhurst, ballplayer, city boy
they dared him take a sauna
climb a bluff, fish, roast a dog
he smiled and took the dares,
he even chopped a log and rowed a boat
he dived into the lake. We toasted the
engagement, glad for such a guy
we'll make him Finnish soon
we swear by rhubarb pie

THE FIGHT

--to Steven

Everyone saw the drama gathering
the fight, explosion soon to come
the sisters in tandem emotion
overly polite in rising tempers
when would they combust?

Denise, Ruth, everyone, knowing, scattered
to the bluff, to Lake Superior,
to the Carnegie Library
to Cedar Lake to swim across
left quick to wait the calm
avoid this ritual fight
but who will make dinner?
the aunts—Mae, Siiri, Tyne
—Suzanne, Ray, Ernie due soon

Steve and Mother
their negotiate natures, thought
"*this* fight again!"
impassioned sisters caught
in an old sibling maze
Steve and Mother saved the family face
 improvised, grilled some tuna, bread,
cut all the summer melon pretty green and red
we reappeared as if on cue
the aunts, Suzanne, arrived to dinner made and due
as always as if nothing's happened

funny Ernie made his horse sounds for the kids
we sat around the table, acting and in fact blessed
the fighting over, sang some show tunes later
 sisterstorm receded, passed, tumult at rest

HER SECRET PLACE

We walk in May in back of rain; new hatch
mosquitoes blur Lake Angeline
Sun gleams on wet green weeds, a tangled thatch
We snap branch switches, slap, and whine
Our small dog scurries by for chippies, mice
Songbirds halt as we come near. Far on some geese
drift northward from the lake, honk twice and thrice.
Upon the bluff my mother sights her secret perch
a place she's cleaned, a cove in rock quite sheer
in mountain ash, oak, sumac, and white birch
"If you miss me, come and find me here."
Imagined knells of bells ring in my inner ear.
I am afraid. My mother must not die!
I joke, "The bugs are killing me." I lie.

EPILOGUE

"The Summer of the Great Blue Herons"
Photo by Jane Piirto

THE SUMMER OF THE GREAT BLUE HERONS

We sit by the side of sand-bottomed Lake Stella, south of Munising, in the evening on a bench. As we softly talk, a Great Blue Heron leaves the reeds on our right and flies, flapping, across our view to the reeds on our left. Kay says, "I have been seeing him a lot. He must have been just behind that point and heard our voices and decided to change places." We watch him highstep through the slim green reeds, silhouetted, bobbing. I say I saw a Great Blue Heron fly across the road to Negaunee, where I have been walking my four miles a day. This was the first time I knew there were Great Blue Herons so close to highway M-28. We comment admiringly on the heron's bulk in the air, the shape of its lumbering flight. The lift reminds me of the flight of ring-necked pheasants in South Dakota that I used to see when field training our Labrador retrievers. We are in our early fifties, two women who've been friends for over twenty-five years, since we were young, pregnant professors together, office mates at Northern Michigan University, instructors in the English department. Now our children are twenty-five years old. We can't believe time has passed so swiftly and that we're so solidly middle-aged.

The next morning, after peevishly complaining about the lack of sun, the fifty degrees cold air, the settling in of a cold front from Canada, the rainstorm that hit at 3 AM, and the possibilities of more rain throughout the day—though the Green Bay station says it will clear—we say the hell with it. Let's just go. Our plan is to canoe two lakes and the Indian River. The wind blows whitecaps on Lake Stella behind Kay as she pulls out the chain from the canoe nestled between a kayak and a rowboat. The boats are securely locked because the camps on Lake Stella have been experiencing break-ins. Such thieves are usually caught at pawnshops or by boasting, Kay's husband, a policeman, has told her.

We heft the canoe up the piny sloping trail, through trees, up to Kay's pickup. Kay climbs up on the bed and we hoist it up onto the canoe supports, placing the styrofoam pads on top of the pickup. She ties the canoe down, front, back, and inside. This aluminum canoe, quite wide and squat, can carry three people comfortably. Kay invited my mother out here for the two nights also, as the three of us have had a comradeship of hiking in the woods for years now, but my mother said she had too much work to do at home (her usual excuse). Kay said my mother could sit in the middle like a queen as we canoe.

I follow Kay the ten miles through long leafy sand and gravel green road tunnels, to Cook's Lake Landing, where we plan to put in, but as we drive into the parking lot we see the whitecaps indicating the fierce winds that will be in our faces, and decide not to do the lakes part of the plan, but just to do the river. I trail her a few more miles to a bridge over the Indian River, and we unload the canoe, leaving it high on the bank while I follow her 2.7 miles down the road to the place we'll end up. We're in the Hiawatha National Forest, and the Indian River is a registered wild river with few improvements, so the signs at both ends warn us of possible debris, as the river isn't a maintained canoe route. On the map it twists like yarn.

Kay parks her Dodge Ram at the bottom of the proposed run, locking it, sticking the keys in the tight front pockets of her jeans. When we get back to the canoe, I park my 78-year-old mother's 1986 stick-shift, four-wheel drive Jimmy, lock it, and Kay pockets my keys also, because I am wearing sweatpants and if we dump, I'm afraid I'll lose the keys in the water. We carry the picnic container containing sandwiches, potato chips, chocolate chip cookies, and bottled water to the canoe landing, as well as a plastic bag with Kay's camera and sunscreen. We slide the canoe down the log skids and pop it into the river. The river is low, slow, about four or five miles an hour, I calculate, remembering the Au Sable River in Lower Michigan, which flows at six miles an hour.

The light brown tannic water lets us see clearly all the way down to the sandy bottom. Kay takes the stern, as she is an experienced canoeist, having done such adventures as Canadian whitewater canoeing a few years ago during the highwater month of May with her brother, and last week, the Boundary Waters of Minnesota with her husband. She describes how her husband carried their canoe, 64 pounds light, on a long portage of over a mile, on his shoulders last week on their vacation in the Boundary Waters, barely breathing hard. We agree it's quite nice to have a fit young husband with whom to portage.

I take the bow, the position I've always had in canoeing with

• The Summer of the Great Blue Herons

my children's father and with various boyfriends over the years, obeying their shouts of "paddle!" "push off!" "other side!" as well as I could in my feminine canoeing clumsiness. Kay says, as I nervously switch sides, "Choose one side and stay there." I choose the left side. It's coming back to me. I haven't canoed for over ten years, except on Helen Lake. "Just warn of boulders, logs, stuff we might hit," says Kay.

I warn of a large black rock with streaming watercress on it, but we sail right over it. I warn of a stump right in the middle and looking near the surface but we sail right over it. The draft on this wide canoe is quite high. We are gliding over obstacles I was sure we would hit. The current carries us along, and we establish a rhythm. I stop warning of the rocks and stumps as we seem to be sailing over them without hitting. We begin to relax and enjoy the scenery, the reeds and swampy land, the overhanging cedars, the fragile hemlocks, feathery tamaracks, solid white pines, birches, maples. There are no fish, though I spot crab-like hellgrammites. Kay says this isn't a fishing river. The river looks quite sterile; its sand bottom is not conducive to trout, which prefer pebbly bottoms I recall from seventeen years of marriage to a fly fisherman, though there are some deep holes where fish would probably like to gather. Periodically snags block the river. Some have been sawed at the deepest part in a three-foot, canoe-sized passageway. We negotiate these timidly at first, and then more confidently. "Push off," Kay says. "Paddle!"

Then we come to a place where a jackpine log fell right across the twenty-foot wide river in a shallow spot. The canoe grinds to a halt, scraping on the pine. We sit high on the barrier, with no way around. This tree obviously fell in quite recently, or the water has dropped. Reluctant to hop in and get wet, we maneuver to the swampy shore, get out, and pull the canoe through the grass, around the log, put in again, and cheer ourselves. A sense of capability, competence, and power overtakes me, a feeling similar to that which I feel driving a sport vehicle or truck on icy roads in winter. I heard a story from a friend where she described how she and two other women took their old teak inboard out in the Les Cheneaux Islands one day, for the first time without a husband to drive; how they figured out how to shift it and how to steer it and how they felt strong and confident as they cut the motor and drifted back in to the dock, wimps no more.

I told Kay on our way back from dropping off the pickup truck, riding over the dirt road in my mother's Jimmy, how much fun this is. How glad I am she suggested it. How grateful I am to her for all the adventures we continue to have, even in our fifties, on the dirt back roads and lakes of the Upper Peninsula. We recall our trip through the logging trails to L'Anse from the McCormick tract on the Peshekee River Grade a few years past, where we negotiated the Jimmy through deep potholes, Kay out front and directing me who had the truck in four-wheel drive, tipping precariously sideways, my mother in the back seat fearfully shouting "No! Turn back! Be careful!"

Now, here on the river, we talk of how women our age just don't seem to be doing such woods adventuring, though we are the generation that started the current wave of women's rights. On their trip to the Boundary Waters, all the women she saw were younger. Kay said when we were hoisting the canoe on the truck, she thought about other close friends, fit, athletic, killers at tennis or racquetball, who would be complaining right about then about how heavy the canoe was, how it hurt the fingers to grip it and the back to carry it and how canoeing wouldn't seem like fun at all. Canoeing or hiking, with bugs, dirt, and risk of tumbling in doesn't seem to appeal to women our age. But when I drive and explore in the woods I feel strength, capability, power. These are often considered masculine words and we feel quite masculine and powerful as we weave our way around the bends and twists of this river, having fun trying to negotiate our way through the challenging snags.

There! to our left. We hear and then see a deer, startled. He leaps and splashes through the river, dashes up the sand bank and disappears. Silently we paddle, naming flowers. Canadian thistle. Wild rose. Beach pea. Blue-stemmed goldenrod. Common mullein. Swamp candles. Common cattail. Yellow hawkweed. Joe-Pye weed.

"I *like* the snags," I say. Kay laughs. We say how relaxing it is not to be yelled at. When we're canoeing with a man in the stern, he always yells, gets excited and angry, has rude tantrums, treats us like incompetent babies. And we feel bad, dumb, foolish. Here today, we calmly give and take directions, and teamwork gets us off the logs, the snags. I tell how a friend and I got lost in Pennsylvania on the way to visit our children in New York City last Christmas, and how we calmly asked directions, took an alternate route, and arrived an hour later, driving at midnight through the Holland Tunnel, viewing the lit skyscrapers of beautiful New York City at Christmas when the city is in its glory, and how she said with her husband, the trip would have become a shouting disaster about the time we took the wrong turn. Kay and I wonder aloud why some men get so upset on road trips and canoe trips. This is a perfect time to pull out the old cliché, "Go with the flow." We laugh. We turn a bend, and spread out before us, the river becomes fifty feet wide, rippling in dappled jeweled sun over pebbles and rocks.

"Go toward the flat water," Kay tells me, and we do, negotiating the slow rapids. "Whitewater is like this, only fifty times worse." I say my sister Ruth can handle whitewater; a canoe instructor, she used to train her girls by taking them over waterfalls when she was a camp counselor. We are laughing, giggling, talking. "Perhaps we should enter a senior citizens' women's canoe race," I brag.

Then—scrape. Grounded again. The wideness and shallowness should have been a warning. We are not ready for the races yet. We push off, push down, push sideways, with the paddles, trying to float ourselves off. No. Finally Kay relents, takes off her shoes and socks, and hops into the water, guiding the canoe to the right bank, to a spot a little deeper, and pushes us off downstream again, stepping deftly back into the stern. After the slow rapids we round another bend and a high bank of snowy birches greets us. In front of us from the reedy bank on the right a Great Blue Heron takes off, flying before us down the valley of the river. He's my third in as many days and like the others, he takes my breath away. He rounds a short bend and disappears. We follow and there he is, in the rushes ahead of us, hiding behind a cluster of bushes. I signal Kay, pointing. We silently approach him, our paddles in our laps, our bodies immobile. We near and again he flies off, pounding, pounding his wings fast, faster, a metal-blue missile with a clumsy sound, his legs trailing off behind him uselessly dangling like bent scaly brown twigs.

This time, as we paddle round the bend, we spot him right away, sort of hunching, hiding, yet alert. We stop paddling and drift toward him again. This time, I see his eye, a whorl in a whirl of feathers, his Elvis Presley cowlick, and even the pupils darting as his head bobs. Then again, swiftly, away, he takes the air down the river in front of us. This begins to resemble a teasing game. He seems curious about us and we are curious about him. Will he let us drift right by him? He seems afraid to fly back over our heads, but prefers to go farther and farther down the river. We round another bend where a small stream enters through reeds and bushes. In a loud clatter, ducks, two of them, with white and brown blurs of tails, take off up the feeder stream into the heart of dark woods. "And a Great Blue Heron," Kay says. He has disappeared into the brushy stream.

We have lost him. We burst into a disagreement. "Yes, it was one duck."

"No, two."

"I just saw one, but the sound is unmistakable. I didn't see a heron."

"Yes, there was too a heron."

But no. There he is, just ahead. He flies up. We are still playing our hide and seek game. Then, around the next corner, a whole paper birch tree has fallen in, a tangle of branches and leaves. We hit it head on, and the river turns us so we are flush against it. The Forest Service hasn't cut this one either, expecting us to duck low as we flow beneath a curve in the trunk near shore. I am pushing off with my hands on the twigs, trying to get a grip to hold us steady. Kay is pushing off the trunk, trying to set the canoe pointed downstream, and then to turn us so the bow will be headed toward the arc in the trunk. We work at opposite intentions, smack up against the branches.

The canoe belches, burps, and slowly rolls over. We have ditched. The water rises to my chest—tippecanoe and Tyler too! I roll out into the water, my light hiking boots hitting the sand bottom so that the water is to my neck. Why hadn't I worn my new aquasocks that I just bought last week for running from the sauna into Helen Lake at camp? My black Sturgis, South Dakota 1993 Motorcycle Classic baseball cap that my artist son and his friends admired during my last visit to his home in Colorado, flows off my ponytail. The cooler floats. The paddle floats. Kay tumbles next to me. We both gulp water and then right ourselves. We hold on to the canoe as it silently fills with water.

"My camera!" I grab her camera case and the plastic bag, filled with water, camera, and sunscreen floating in the filled canoe. The water is surprisingly warm, I notice. August. Thank God the water isn't cold, I think. It's in the high sixties, I register.

"The paddle!" "The cushions!" she shouts, or I do. But

we calmly guide the canoe to the opposite bank, ducking below the birch snag and beach the canoe there. I struggle back for the canoe paddle floating, serenely bobbing, behind a catch on a twig. She grabs my floating hat. We stand there, thigh deep in water and ankle deep in muck, and laugh. Since we swim across northern lakes together most summers, neither of us has experienced fear of drowning in this overturn. I can barely step, the bottom is so suckingly mucky. My boots sink slowly. I struggle, lean, slurp the foot from the muck. We dump it in the middle of the stream and take it back to shore. "One, two, three, turn it," one of us says. The canoe again rides high.

We beach it in the reeds and I take my place on my green cushion in the front, put back there from where Kay has rescued it from downstream about fifty feet, caught in an eddy. Kay retrieves the paddle hidden in grassy reeds, and steps in, pushing us off, wet, soaked, heavy with water, but laughing. "The water was warmer than I thought," I say in a chesty watery voice, from beneath my layers of wet bra,wet t-shirt, wet sweatshirt, wet sweater, wet poncho, wet sweat pants, wet socks, wet underpants, wet light hiking boots. "I'm glad I left my Timex watch back at camp."

Kay, the optimist, had left her expensive watch on, and it is stopped. Three o'clock. The dumping hour. August 9. Two fifty-year old canoeists, soaking wet. "It's not much farther," Kay says. She is shivering and her teeth chatter, as she is much thinner than I, and doesn't have the layer of protective fat that I do. I am not very cold at all within my dripping layers. She gets and puts on a blue plastic bag from the cooler, and feels warmer. We are sure our mishap has scared off our new heron friend, but no.

As we round the next bend, he appears, to the right, in front, as if he has been waiting for us. We quiet down from our gasping laughter and chills, and seriously and silently drift toward him. He turns downstream and embarks into the afternoon air, pounding his way around the next bend. Neither of us has seen a Great Blue Heron so close as he is letting us come. He does this a few more times—about eight or ten times total, we figure later. We hear another deer thrashing about in the brush, pass through more cedar swamps, see more birch patches and dramatic white pines leaning out over the banks. The chill is leaving Kay as she paddles, steering us.

The river has more rewards for us as we spot a belted kingfisher diving straight down into a pool from a high dead cedar branch. Kingfishers seem to be fearless, as they hurtle themselves into the water, almost as brash as pairs of brown pelicans doing tandem diving. The kingfisher circles back and checks us out and then soars off. The distance is longer than we think. Kay makes me promise not to tell Ted, as he will make fun of her, of us.

I promise not to, but this is another good woods adventure in our history of such expeditions (the time we got lost and had to slide down high, rocky, weedy power line right-of-ways on our rear ends was a good one, too; we ate thimbleberries all the way down) and I don't promise not to tell my journal, or my other friends. I'm sure it's such a good story she will tell him, though she vows not to. We round one more bend and there it is, the red pickup parked high above the river. We put in, clamber out, and pull/push the canoe up the steep log-stepped path, boost it on to the pickup, working quickly, efficiently, a team. We hope our heron friend is back there in the bushes, saying goodbye. Kay begins shivering again, uncontrollably. She secures the front and back ropes and jumps into the cab of the truck, where the heater is running warm air, and eagerly opens the cooler.

"I'm starved." She unwinds the plastic wrap from the hefty tuna fish salad sandwiches on three-grain bread from Sweetwater's in Marquette, and we discover that the sandwiches are dry. They have survived the dumping. We eat ravenously as we drive upstream to the Jimmy. The keys have survived also, and I unlock the truck and follow Kay back to camp. As we strip naked, hanging our heavy, sandy clothes on the railings of the deck, we hasten because we are older now, colder, damper, but also powerful, competent, strong.

Sitting in front of the fire piled with logs, drinking hot chocolate, luxuriating in our dry clothes, waiting for the marshmallows to melt, we tell the story again and again. We look the birds up in Peterson and the flowers in Audubon. We describe how this *ardea herodias*, length 38 inches, width 70 inches, let us get so close we could see the feathers ruffling in the wind on his colonial blue folded-up wings before his transcendent takeoffs. We decide that this summer will be for us, the summer of the Great Blue Herons.

• • •

ABOUT THE AUTHOR:

JANE PIIRTO was born and raised in Ishpeming, in Marquette County, Michigan, granddaughter of four Finnish immigrants. Her mother is an artist and her father was a welder for the Cleveland Cliffs Iron Company in the brownstone shops. Piirto graduated from Ishpeming High School and attended two Upper Peninsula colleges, Suomi College and Northern Michigan University, from which she received a B.A. in English.

Winner of two Individual Artist Fellowships (in poetry and in fiction) from the Ohio Arts Council, author of the award-winning novel, The Three-Week Trance Diet *(Carpenter Press)*, author of two nonfiction books, Understanding Those Who Create *(Ohio Psychology Press) and* Talented Children and Adults *(Macmillan), of two poetry chapbooks,* mamamama *(Sisu Press) and* Postcards from the Upper Peninsula *(Pocasse Press), she has master's degrees from Kent State University and South Dakota State University and a Ph.D. from Bowling Green State University. An educator, she has been a high school teacher, a poet in the schools, a college professor, a guidance counselor, a coordinator of county and regional education programs in Michigan, South Dakota, and Ohio. She is a former principal of the Hunter College Campus Schools in New York City. Jane is currently Professor of Teacher Education at Ashland University, Ashland, Ohio. She has two grown children and frequently visits the Upper Peninsula.*